CONTENTS

IN THIS BOOK
– Info on ingredients and cooking instructions

Ingredients show the minimum amount to make 1 portion unless specified. Adjust the amount according to the size of your bento box or the number of servings you will need.

Measuring tools used in the recipes are based on the following: 1 cup = 240 ml, 1 Tablespoon (Tbsp) = 15 ml, 1 teaspoon (tsp) = 5 ml

Microwave cooking is based on 500W setting. If using 600W setting, reduce the suggested time by 20%, or multiply by 0.8.

Toaster oven cooking time depends on manufacturer and model. Adjust the time by checking the doneness through the glass window.

Rice amount in each bento is based on 2/3 cup (4 oz /115 g) cooked plain rice. Adjust according to your children's needs.

Dashi stock is generally made from *kombu* and dried bonito shavings, but to save time, *dashi* granules are recommended for bento preparations. Reconstitute them with hot water following the directions on the package. When the recipe calls for soy sauce and sugar together with *dashi* stock, *Tsuyu no moto* (noodle sauce) does a great job, also by reconstituting with water.

Rice wine adds fragrance to food, making it mild in flavor. If unavailable, sweet white wine or dry sherry can be substituted for it.

Mirin, or sweet rice wine for cooking, is a kind of thick "*sake*" made by fermenting distilled spirits, glutinous rice and rice malt. It gives mild sweetness to food as well as glaze. Substitutes include sweet sherry or sugar syrup mixed with rice wine.

Bento box dividers such as green leaves are not included in the ingredients. Neither are decorations like parsley sprigs. You can substitute anything you have on hand.

BENTO BASICS

BENTO BOX ENERGY

Calorie-wise, lunch for school goers should supply 500 to 700 Cal per portion. To reduce calories just reduce the amount of rice/bread/pasta. Remember that 1 oz (30 g) cooked rice gives about 50 Cal while 1 oz (30 g) bread (1 roll or 1 thin slice of bread) gives about 90 Cal.

BEST NUTRITION BALANCE

Amount by Volume

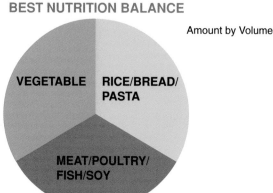

VEGETABLE

RICE/BREAD/PASTA

MEAT/POULTRY/FISH/SOY

ENERGY SOURCE
RICE/BREAD/PASTA

Carbohydrates occupy an important place in the diet as a fast energy source. It is especially essential for children because of their highly active body function. Rice is mostly used in this book, using ²/₃ cup (4 oz /115 g: 200 Cal) cooked rice per portion. Adjust it to individual needs, ideally 1 cup at the most, to fill ¹/₃ to ¹/₂ of the bento box. When mixed with other ingredients, the volume will go up to ²/₃.

BODY BUILDER
MEAT/POULTRY/FISH/SOY

A good supply of protein helps in making bones, muscles and blood. Soybean products such as *tofu*, *aburaage* and *miso* supply isoflavone, known as an antioxidant. You can simply utilize the leftovers from yesterday's dinner by being creative and giving them a makeover. For example, slice meat and vegetable leftovers and add to make a Spanish omelet, or fry them with rice. It is highly recommended to divide the leftovers into small portions and freeze them for later use. Use 2 to 3 oz (60 to 90 g) of items from this category per portion.

BODY TUNER
VEGETABLE/SEA VEGETABLE/MUSHROOM

Vitamins, minerals and dietary fiber maintain the healthy functioning of your body. Combine pale vegetables and colorful, carotene rich vegetables for a balanced diet. Fruits and fruit jelly can be included in this category. Be sure to use at least a 2 oz (60 g) serving from this category per portion.

SMART BENTO PACKING

Pack in a **shallow** container!

If the box is not fully packed, the food items will move around during transport, and look unappetizing to the eater. Be sure to fill the box so the foods abut each other so they do not move.

❶ SET RICE
Fill ¹/₃ of the container with warm rice (cold rice is hard to pack evenly). Leave bento box open to cool.

❷ FIXED SHAPE FOOD
Food that has unchangeable shape such as deep-fried food should be put in first.

❸ JUICY FOOD
Salads or moist food such as cucumber salad, shown here, should be drained well before filling in a deep waterproof container, kept separate from the rest.

HOW TO MAKE LUNCH FUN AND NUTRITIOUS

Keep the following points in mind when planning your bento:

VARIETY OF COLOR

Check the color chart on pages 66 to 75 to make a bento balanced in color and nutrition.

VARIETY OF FLAVOR

Use different tastes and seasonings. Create a good balance of salty, sweet and sour foods, varying the saltiness of each if possible so the eaters can enjoy all of these flavors in one meal. Of course children will love the bento that includes a sweet dessert or fruit.

EASE OF EATING

Be sure to make bite-size food except rice balls which can be held in the hand. It is a good idea to use party picks or skewers for hard to hold finger foods.

COOKING METHODS

Baked, fried, simmered, steamed, boiled, or fresh, there are lots of cooking methods to use. Do not stick to one method, but combine foods cooked different ways. It will automatically create a variety of flavors and textures.

DRAIN AND DIVIDE

Sauced items and salads should be drained well and segregated. Remove excess moisture with a paper towel, if necessary. Use dividers or small containers deep enough to hold these foods. Drippings from food will spoil the flavor of other foods.

KAWAII ARRANGEMENT

You do not have to spend too much time, but try to draw the kid's appetite and interest. Just change the shape of rice balls or sandwiches as well as varying the shapes of sliced ingredients.

SAFE PACKING

Pack food items to abut each other to avoid moving and mixing. Check the color chart on pages 66 to 75 to make a bento balanced in color and nutrition. Use handy bento box fillers shown below to ensure tight packing.

SEASON WELL

Remember that the bento will be completely cooled when eaten. Since warm food tastes better, consider using a bit more seasoning to flavor your choices.

Handy Bento Fillers

Dried fruit

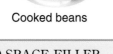
Cooked beans

Mini jellies
(Agar-agar Jellies)

Dried savories

Wrapped cheese

---

❹ SHAPABLE FOOD
Food that can be slightly squashed such as vegetable omelet should be added at this point.

❺ SPACE FILLER
Fill any space with preserved food such as simmered red beans shown here. Cherry tomatoes, pickles, fruit and sauce containers always work well for this purpose. Check the color chart (p 66-75) to make a complete meal.

❻ FINISH
Enhance the plain rice with *nori* or rice sprinkles. Add charming party picks, where necessary.

❼ COOL COMPLETELY BEFORE REPLACING LID
The steam from warm food may make the food soggy, and most importantly, make it perishable at warm temperature.

HOW TO CHOOSE BENTO BOXES AND GEAR

BENTO BOXES

Compared to regular sealing containers such as Tupperware, a small bento box can hold an unexpectedly large volume of food because it should be tightly packed to avoid mixing. You can choose from various shapes, materials and sizes. For younger school kids, one that holds $1^1/_2$ to 2 cups (450 to 500 ml) is average, and for young elementary school kids you need up to 3 cup (700 ml) containers. Roughly speaking, the bento box capacity often suggests the calorie content itself. Be careful so as not to use oversized container for your kid.

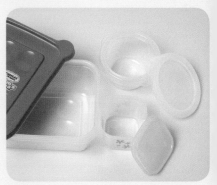

Slim, oval shaped boxes, often 2-tiered or 3-tiered, are the most popular type as they safely "sit" at the bottom of school bags. After eating, smaller tiers often fit into the largest tier for carrying.

For bento beginners, a box with compartments or dividers is easy to pack as it prevents the foods from mingling with each other. A 2-tiered box with side locks is convenient for sauced food.

Containers with air-tight seals are perfect for desserts or sauced food items. Every household should have one.

RICE BALL MOLDS

Just fill with rice and press, and voila! Cute faces will smile at the eater. Since the rice is packed, a good amount of rice will be supplied especially for light eaters.

CUTTERS

Cookie cutters can be used to cut out sandwiches, thin egg omelets and vegetables. Use a small size ice cream scoop for shaping potato salad or mixed rice.

FOOD PICKS

A cute accessory that is both practical and colorful. Sausages, meatballs and boiled quail eggs are easy to eat with party picks, but they may occupy too much space in a small bento box. Be sure not to use very short ones for young preschoolers.

MINI FOOD CUPS

To segregate each food item, these small cups are a must. Cooking method may differ depending on the material : Glassine paper cups are microwave friendly, crisp plastic cups are for soft desserts while aluminum cups are for baking in a toaster oven. Silicone baking cups would work for all these purposes.

DIVIDERS

Modern versions of natural leaf dividers used in Japanese dishes. Green "grass" dividers are often seen in sushi bento, and many cute designs can be found nowadays. Some dividers can be rolled and set to use as mini cups. Adjust to the height of bento box by folding or trimming the bottom part.

MINI SAUCE BOTTLES

For liquid sauces like soy sauce or dressing, choose one with a narrow mouth. Bottles with a wide cap are useful for thick sauces like ketchup or mayonnaise. Noodles to be eaten dipped in sauce (page 42) requires a larger bottle to hold enough sauce to pour over the noodles. Check if the cap can be fixed and removed easily and safely.

HOW TO COOK RICE THE JAPANESE WAY

Plain white rice goes with nearly every dish, and if you have mastered Japanese style rice cooking, you can make tasty moist rice balls, and easily go on to making delicious sushi rice quickly at home.
Use short grain rice, and account for the cooking time as it will take 30 to 40 minutes at least. Expect to add that amount of time to bento preparation time.

Plain rice tastes best when cooked in a large batch. So, cook the maximum quantity of rice in your rice cooker or pot, and freeze for later use. It is recommended to divide the rice into portions while hot, and wrap each portion in a flat square shape before freezing, making sure not to press excessively. This way the rice will stay fluffy after being thawed. The microwave oven is a perfect tool to thaw the rice. Set at high heat and check the doneness after 2 minutes per portion ($\frac{2}{3}$ cup).

RINSING RICE

If using prewashed rice, omit the washing process, but be sure to use a reduced cup size for rice and water measurement. In either case, use an equal amount of rice and water.

1. Measure out the rice into a large bowl. Add water to cover, and quickly rub the grains swishing them around with your hands, for about 3 seconds. Immediately discard the milky white water.

2. Add water again and repeat, this time taking more time. Repeat several times until the water runs almost clear.

3. Drain the rice in a colander, and let stand 30 minutes to 1 hour, if possible.

COOKING RICE

A rice cooker cooks perfect rice without any effort, and keeps the rice warm until actual use. It is worth investing in, but you can cook the rice in a pot as well with a little attention.

Rice Cooker

1. Place rinsed and drained rice in the inner pot of the cooker. Add water up to the appropriate marking line of the pot. Let rice soak 30 minutes, or turn on immediately.

2. When cooking is over, it automatically switches to keep-warm mode. Using the attached non-stick paddle, fluff rice lightly.

NOTES ON WATER RATIO

The ratio of rice to water is not fixed. Generally, if cooking very small amount of rice, more water is needed than when cooking a large batch. Refer to the table below to check for the right proportions.

DESIRED COOKED RICE	TO COOK	
	Raw Rice	Water
2$\frac{1}{2}$ cups	1 cup	1$\frac{1}{4}$ cups
5 cups	2 cups	2-2$\frac{1}{4}$ cups
7$\frac{1}{2}$ cups	3 cups	3-3$\frac{1}{4}$ cups

* Use about 100-120 % amount of water to uncooked rice, depending on the condition of the rice used. If using old rice, add some extra water for a soft finish.
* For sushi rice, less cooking water is required than usual as vinegar will be added later.
* The rice increases by 130% in weight when cooked.

Pot

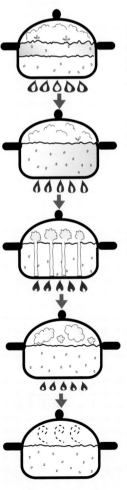

1. Use a medium pot with heavy bottom and tight lid. Place measured and rinsed rice in the pot. Add an equal amount of water. Cover and cook 5-6 minutes over very high heat until boiling.

2. Reduce heat to medium high, and cook 1 minute. Be careful not to boil over.

3. Reduce heat to medium, and cook 7-8 minutes.

4. Reduce heat to very low, and cook for 15 minutes. Keep covered.

5. Turn off heat, and let steam 10 minutes, covered. Fluff with the attached paddle while hot.

RICE BALL (ONIGIRI) BENTO

Onigiri or *omusubi* is always a children's favorite bento component, and its variations are endless. Even a young preschooler can eat these with no difficulty. Enjoy designing your own *onigiri*.

menu
Just Us *Onigiri* (see below)
Fried Chicken (see p 56)
Rolled Omelet (see p 61)
Cooked Asparagus
Cherry Tomato

> **Hint:** *Nori* eyes are useful to use with any type of food. Make a number of eyes using a hole punch and stock them for busy mornings.

JUST US BENTO

How to make Just Us *Onigiri*

* Make a flat, round *onigiri* with about 2 oz (60 g) warmed rice.

Common: ❶❷ Boy: ❸❹❺ Girl: ❸❹❺

❶ Place filling (salmon flakes) in the center of rice.
❷ With both of your hands, form a flattened ball.
❸ Cut 3 "hair" strips of *nori* seaweed, and stick to the rice.
❹ Cut nori into a strip as wide as onigiri height, and wrap upper half.
❺ Position *nori* eyes and mouth of trimmed pickled plum.
❸ Stick two *nori* squares as bangs.
❹ Cut *nori* into a strip as wide as *onigiri* height, and wrap upper half.
❺ Position *nori* eyes and mouth of trimmed pickled plum.

ONIGIRI FRIENDS

A cute animal face or favorite item can be a lunchtime star. To attach cheese slices, use a dab of mayonnaise as a glue. Place in a container to keep the shape.

MR. SMILEY

On a flat, round *onigiri*, attach round cheeks and nose with cut-out crisp, small pickled plum, and attach eyebrows, eyes and mouth with cut-out *nori* sheet.

SAMURAI MAN

On a flat, triangular *onigiri*, attach *nori* for hair and side burns, and then eyes, eyebrows and mouth. Cut out mouth shape from crisp, small pickled plum.

SOCCER BALL

Lay a sheet of *nori* flat, and using a sharp knife cut out hexagons and very narrow strips. Arrange them over a ball shaped *onigiri*.

PANDA

Form a rough hexagon *onigiri*, and attach *nori* eyes and nose. Cut out large ears from *nori*, and wrap a tiny amount of rice inside to shape ears.

PIGLET

Mix warmed rice with salmon flakes, and form an oval *onigiri*. Press in carrot ears and mouth, and attach cheese nose and *nori* eyes.

FROGGY

Mix warmed rice with any minced greens, and form an oval *onigiri*. Attach cheese and *nori* eyes. Attach carrot or red pepper mouth.

PUPPY

Make a flat, egg shaped *onigiri*, and attach sausage nose and ears (using snack noodle sticks). Stick *nori* eyes and scatter black sesame seeds for whiskers.

CAT

On a flat, round *onigiri*, attach fish sausage ears using snack noodle sticks. Cut out eyes and whiskers from *nori*, and nose and mouth from crisp, small pickled plum.

menu

Triangular _Onigiri_ (see below)
Fried Prawns (see p 57 and add a bottle of tartar sauce)
Squash Salad (see p71)
Spaghetti "Napolitan" (see p 40 and add sausage)

Hint: Since rice is stickier when it is hot or warm, rice balls can be shaped more easily with it. If using cold rice, microwave until hot.

CLASSIC ONIGIRI COMBO

How to make Triangular _Onigiri_   * Use about 2 oz (60 g) cooked rice per ball.

1 Place filling (_furikake/_ rice sprinkles - see p 81) in the center of rice.

2 Bring rice around the edges to cover the filling.

3 Wet your hands with heavily salted water. Flatten the bottom side with your left hand while shaping a triangular corner with right hand. Rotate and repeat on each side to form a triangle.

4 Wrap _onigiri_ with a _nori_ sheet strip. Finish with toasted sesame seeds sprinkled over white rice.

menu
Fried Chicken *Onigiri*
 (see p 56 for Fried Chicken and Hint below)
Spinach with *Nametake* Mushrooms
 (see p 67)
Ham Stuffed Cherry Tomatoes
 (see p 69)
Boiled Egg (Sprinkle with *Gomashio*,
 or toasted sesame seeds and salt)
Baby Apple Rabbit (see P 65)

Hint: Referring to bottom of previous page, wrap a piece of fried chicken with rice, shaping into a round *onigiri*.

FRIED CHICKEN ONIGIRI COMBO

TEN-MUSU (TEMPURA ONIGIRI) BENTO

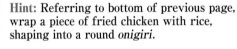

menu
Prawn *Tempura Onigiri* (see below)
Rolled *Nori* and Cheese Omelet
 (see p 61 and roll with a *nori* sheet and sliced cheese)
Boiled Broccoli
Sweet Potato and Carrot *Tempura* (see below)
Strawberries

Prawn *Tempura Onigiri*

Shell and devein prawns. Make batter by combining water, beaten egg and all purpose flour in a ratio of 1 : 1 : 2. Dust prawns with salt and flour, and dip in the batter. Heat vegetable oil to 350°F/180℃ and deep-fry prawns until golden. Referring to bottom of previous page, wrap a fried prawn with rice, shaping into a triangular *onigiri*.

Sweet Potato and Carrot *Tempura*

Cut potato and carrot into strips. Make batter by combining water, beaten egg and all purpose flour in a ratio of 1 : 1 : 2. Add vegetable strips into batter. Taking 5-7 mixed strips, drop in 320°F (160℃) vegetable oil and deep-fry until crisp.

menu
Cannon Ball *Onigiri*
 (see below)
Okra with Bonito Shavings
 (see p 67)
Ground Beef with *Gobo*
 (see p 74)
Sausages
Cherry Tomato
Agar-agar Jelly
Canned Satsuma

Taste good!

CANNON BALL BENTO

How to make Triangular *Onigiri*

✳ For a change, use a cheese ball or cube →

1

Lay plastic wrap on a surface. Spread warm rice over it.

2

Place a meatball in the center.

3

Bring all sides of the plastic wrap, and twist them at the top so a ball shape is formed.

4

Unwrap and cover the rice with *nori*, torn into small pieces. Small pieces are recommended since a large sheet of *nori* will have folds and won't wrap around the ball nicely.

menu

Wrapped *Onigiri* (see below)
Spinach with Black Sesame Dressing
 (see p 66 and save some for *onigiri*)
Rolled Omelet (see p 61)
Strawberries
Kiwi Fruit
Cheese Balls (commercial)

Wrapped *Onigiri*

Mix half portion of rice with *yukari* (red *shiso* sprinkles - see p 81). On plastic wrap, place crispy pickled plum cut into shapes. Then add mixed rice. Referring to bottom of previous page, wrap up into round ball. For plain rice *onigiri*, arrange spinach stems and slice of *naruto* (fishcake - see p 81) to resemble flower. Carefully place rice over it, and form a ball in the same manner.

WRAPPED ONIGIRI COMBO

HAWAIIAN MUSUBI BENTO

menu

Hawaiian *Musubi* (see below)
Pineapple Salad (see p 71)
Boiled Egg (add mayonnaise)
Potato Chips
Cherry Tomato

Hawaiian *Musubi*

Cut Spam into thick slices, adjusting to size for bento box used. Using warm rice, make oblong rice balls to fit to Spam slices. Press Spam slice onto rice, and wrap center with a *nori* strip.

Hint: Try with sliced corned beef or fish sausage.

menu
Molded *Onigiri* (see below)
Sausage Sunflowers (see below)
Potato Stir Fry (see p 72)
Baby Apple Rabbit (see p 65)

15

Molded *Onigiri*

Make bear face with *nori*, and add *furikake* (rice sprinkles - see p 81) onto ears. Make rabbit eyes and mouth with imitation crab stick, and ears with pink *dembu* (fish flakes - see p 81).

Sausage Sunflowers

Split sausage vertically into halves. Slit deeply along edges and join ends with toothpick. Place on a frying pan, and drop a quail egg in the center and cook.

MOLDED ONIGIRI COMBO

How to make Molded *Onigiri*
* Use about 2 oz (60 g) cooked rice per *onigiri*.

1

Blanch mold for easy unmolding. Pack it with rice.

2

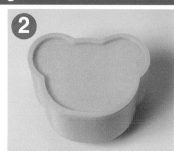

Close the lid firmly.

3

Turn over and unmold.

4

Wet your hands with heavily salted water, and arrange the shape. Attach features.

Skewered *Onigiri*

Using a piece of plastic wrap, form small rice balls in the same manner as page 10. Unwrap and arrange the shape with your hands wet with heavily salted water. Make 6 and coat each with black and white ground sesame seeds, and *aonori* (green *nori* flakes) to make two of each color. Skewer them to fit into the bento box.

Tri-color Meatballs

Make meatballs referring to page 55. Over a piece of plastic wrap, spread minced string beans evenly, and sprinkle with flour. Center uncooked meatball, and wrap it with string bean pieces. Twist the top. In the same manner, make meatballs with sweet corn and minced red bell pepper. Microwave 2 minutes each.

> **Hint:** Small ball-shaped food items are easy to eat and fun to look at.

(from left to right)
string beans
corn
red bell pepper

menu

Skewered *Onigiri* (see left)
Tri-color Meatballs (see p 55 and see left for coating)
Cherry Tomato
Dried Tuna Cubes

SKEWERED ONIGIRI COMBO WITH TASTY COATING

TEDDY ONIGIRI COMBO

menu

Molded Teddy *Onigiri* (see below)
Croquettes
(frozen product, thawed)
Kimpira (see p 75)
Boiled Broccoli
Cheese Ball
Satsuma

Molded Teddy *Onigiri*

Cut out *nori* into squares and circles to make eyes and mouths. Cut out bows from crispy pickled plum to make ties. Stick them in position. Press *furikake* (rice sprinkles - see p 81) or sesame seeds onto each body to resemble clothes.

> **Hint:** Add favorite fillings to *onigiri*, or use mixed rice for a change.

13

menu

Treasure Bags (see below)
Bacon-rolled Asparagus (see p 66)
Fluffy Potatoes (see p 72)
Strawberries

TREASURE BAG ONIGIRI COMBO

Treasure Bag Filling (Chicken Rice)

$^2/_3$ cup (4 oz /115 g) cooked rice
1 oz (30 g) chicken, minced
$^1/_4$ onion, minced
1 Tbsp minced carrot and bell pepper
1 Tbsp ketchup
Dash salt

Stir-fry minced chicken and vegetables until chicken is heated through. Add rice and stir-fry 1 minute, then stir in ketchup. Add salt to taste. Using plastic wrap, shape into 2 balls.

How to make Treasure Bag

Make thin omelet. Combine 1 egg, 1 tsp sugar and pinch of salt, and pour half portion into a greased frying pan. Cook over low heat. Do not turn over. Make 2.

Remove omelet to plastic wrap set on a dish, and center the ball of chicken rice.

Bring all sides of the wrap to the top to wrap up the rice. Bind the top with a twist tie.

Fried Rice *Onigiri*

$2/3$ cup (4 oz /115g) cooked rice,
$1/4$ onion, chopped,
1 oz (30 g) shrimp, 1 egg, beaten
1 tsp each chopped carrot and
sugar peas, 1 tsp soy sauce,
Dash salt

1. Make fried rice. Make scrambled egg with a dash of salt, in a greased frying pan. Remove and cool.
2. Add vegetable oil to the pan, and stir-fry carrot, onion and shrimp.
3. Add rice, scrambled egg and sugar peas. Stir well to mix, over high heat. Add soy sauce and salt to taste.
4. Over a piece of plastic wrap, place a portion of fried rice. Bring up all sides of the wrap and twist them to make a ball.

Hint: Rice balls made of fried rice are not easy to eat with a fork or chopsticks. Make fail-proof *onigiri* using plastic wrap.

menu
Fried Rice *Onigiri* (see left)
Bean-thread Vermicelli Salad (see p 73)
Sausage Octopus (see p 63)
Milk Jelly (see p 76)

WRAPPED FRIED RICE ONIGIRI COMBO

HIJIKI ONIGIRI COMBO

menu
Hijiki* Seaweed *Onigiri (see below)
Fried Prawns (see p 57)
Skewered cherry tomatoes and cucumber
Persimmon Wedges

Hijiki Seaweed *Onigiri*

Make Simmered *Hijiki* Seaweed referring to page 74. Cut up simmered *hijiki* and mix it with $2/3$ cup (4 oz /115 g) cooked rice, and shape into 2 round rice balls. Wrap sides with *nori* strips.

Hint: If *inari-zushi* pouches (see p 28) are available, pack them with the rice for more flavor.

15

CREATIVE RICE BENTO IDEAS

Rice can be arranged in many ways. You can make flavorful mixed or fried rice in no time. You can create a "picture" over the packed rice, or make a *"donburi"* with tasty toppings. Surprise your kid with a fanciful display on a special day.

menu

Teddy Bear Rice (see below)
Heart Shaped Omelet (see p 61)
Meatballs (see p 55)
Boiled Broccoli
Milk Jelly (see p 76)
Strawberries

TEDDY BEAR BENTO

How to make Teddy Bear Rice

1 Make a thin omelet referring to page 14. Let cool and cut out the shape using a template, cookie cutter, or freehand.

2 Place the shape over the packed rice. Make holes with a hole punch, if preferred.

3 Stick *nori* seaweed cutouts for eyes and mouth. Cut out half circle from a slice of ham and place on the ears.

4 Cover the bear's face and sprinkle with rice sprinkles of your choice over the rice.

INSECT BENTO

Over plain rice, arrange Meat *Soboro* (see p 60), shredded omelet (see p 14) and shredded cucumber or cooked and shredded pea pods. Place Sausage Beetle (see p 63) and Cherry Tomato Ladybug (see p 64) on top.

BUNNY BENTO

Over plain rice, lay cut-out thin omelet (see p 14). Color bunny face with pink *dembu* (fish flakes - see p 81) and position *nori* eyes and carrot mouth. Add parsley and cut-out slices of Glazed Carrot (see p 68).

MARINE BENTO

Mix plain rice with minced pickled greens or rice sprinkles. Cut a trapezoid and a small rectangle out of thin omelet (see p 14). Arrange them to make a ship body, and trim with imitation crab stick (see p 81) and cooked asparagus slices. Arrange *shio kombu* (salted kelp) waves and carrot or corn smoke.

LITTLE GIRL BENTO

Over plain rice, arrange trimmed cheese slice, shredded *nori* hair and eyes, fish sausage mouth and collar, and pink *dembu* (fish flakes - see p 81) cheeks.

OMELET RICE BENTO

How to make Omelet Rice

1 Make Chicken Rice referring to page 14. Melt butter in a frying pan of the same size as your bento container. Beat 1 egg, and pour into the pan. Stir just once and leave until half set.

2 Place Chicken Rice as shown.

3 Reduce heat. Using a turner, fold the omelet almost in half.

4 Transfer the omelet into container so the bottom side of the omelet shows. "Draw" pattern with ketchup, or fill a squeezable bottle with ketchup.

Dry Curry

2 oz (60 g) ground beef or pork,
2 Tbsp each minced onion and
carrot, ²/₃ cup (4 oz /115g) cooked
rice, 1 Tbsp each curry powder and
ketchup, ¼ chicken bouillon cube,
1 tsp raisins, Salt and pepper,
1 tsp vegetable oil, Potato chips

1. In a small saucepan or frying
pan, sauté minced onion and carrot,
and then add ground meat. Stir
and cook until the meat is heated
through.
2. Add curry powder, ketchup, 2
Tbsp water, bouillon and raisins.
Simmer until the liquid is gone. Add
salt and pepper to taste.
3. Crush potato chips and mix with
the rice. Place in bento box, and
make a dent along center. Fill it
with dry curry.

〈Microwave Version〉
1. In a microwave safe container,
combine ground meat and all the
other ingredients. Loosely cover
with plastic wrap, and microwave 3
minutes.
2. Remove the wrap. If the
mixture is too runny, stir once and
microwave again for 3 minutes,
uncovered.

menu
Dry Curry (see left)
Boiled Broccoli
Stuffed *Shiitake* Mushrooms
(see p 74)
Fruit Salad (see p 76)

Hint: Sliced almonds
or cereals also give
the rice crunchiness.

DRY CURRY BENTO

FRIED RICE BENTO

menu
Chinese Fried Rice (see below)
Beef and Pepper Stir Fry
 (see p 67)
Marinated Yellow Bell Pepper
(see p 71)
Cherry Tomatoes
Satsuma

Chinese Fried Rice

²/₃ cup (4 oz /115g) warm rice,
1 egg, 2 slices barbecued pork,
3" (8 cm) green onion, 1" (2.5 cm)
carrot, 1 tsp vegetable oil, Dash
salt, soy sauce and sesame oil

1. Beat the egg and make scrambled
egg; remove. Mince barbecued pork,
green onion and carrot and add
to frying pan greased with ½ tsp
vegetable oil.

2. Cook and stir until supple, and
add rice. When the rice grains are
separated, put back the scrambled
egg. Add dash of salt and soy sauce
to taste. Garnish with *beni-shoga*
(pickled ginger), if preferred.

menu

Mixed Rice (see below)
Boiled Quail Egg Tulips (see below for coloring)
Boiled Pea Pods
Sausage Pineapples (see below)
Broccoli and Salty _Kombu_ (see p 67)
Agar-agar Jelly
Canned Satsuma

Mixed Rice
Mince pickled greens and combine with cooked rice.

Sausage Pineapples
Score lattice pattern on sausage skin, and thrust parsley sprig.

BLOOMING TULIP BENTO

How to make Colored Eggs

Dilute red food coloring in lukewarm water, and soak boiled quail eggs for about 3 minutes, turning over if necessary.

Pat dry. Using a paring knife, make a zigzag incision into egg white. Remove top and arrange on packed rice. Make leaves with diagonally cut pea pods.

Make yellow tulip likewise, using yellow food coloring. Red soaking liquid from _beni-shoga_, or pickled _ginger_, can be used to dye (soak 5 more minutes), and yellow liquid from _takuwan_, or pickled _daikon_ radish, can be used as well.

Mixed Rice (see below)
Vegetable Egg Drops (see below)
Spaghetti "Napolitan" (see p 40)
Cherry Tomato
Kiwi Fruit

Mixed Rice

Combine 2 Tbsp cut up Ground Beef with *Gobo* (see p 74) and ⅔ cup (4 oz /115 g) warm rice. Place in bento box, and add toppings such as sugar peas and corn kernels.

> Hint: Mixed or seasoned rice always enhances the appetite. Just cut up any leftover food and toss with rice.

Veggie Scrambled Egg

Beat 1 egg with salt and pepper. Melt butter in a frying pan, and pour in the mixture. Stir in frozen vegetable mix.

MIXED RICE BENTO

GINGER SCALLOP BENTO

menu

Mixed Rice
  (mix rice with salmon flakes)
Ginger Scallops (see below)
Buttered Corn Egg Drops (see p 71)
Boiled Asparagus (cook with salt)
Cherry Tomatoes

Ginger Scallops

Place 3 small boiled scallops (whole or trimmed), 1 Tbsp each rice wine, *mirin* and soy sauce in a small sauce pan. Simmer until the liquid is thickened and almost gone, and stir in shredded fresh ginger root just before removing from heat. Let cool.

> **Hint:** Salmon flakes are convenient to make rice balls (p 6, p 7) and rice topping (p 25, p 60). They are sold in jars at Japanese food stores and in the international foods aisle of your grocery store.

Chicken *Teriyaki Donburi*
1 small chicken thigh (3-4 oz /90-115 g)
¹/₂ Tbsp each sugar and soy sauce
1 Tbsp rice wine
²/₃ cup (4 oz /115 g) warm rice
Shredded *nori* seaweed

menu
Chicken *Teriyaki Donburi* (see below)
Macaroni Salad (see p 72)
Apple Tulips (see p 65)
Persimmon Wedges

Hint: To make *yakitori*, cut up chicken and cook with the same seasonings, stirring constantly. Skewer 3-4 pieces.

CHICKEN TERIYAKI BENTO

How to make Chicken *Teriyaki Donburi*

❶ In a preheated non-stick frying pan, place chicken thigh skin side down, and cook until browned.

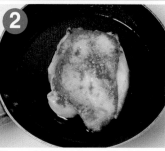
❷ Turn chicken over and add sugar, soy sauce and rice wine. Cover and reduce heat. Cook until the chicken is heated through.

❸ Remove lid. Turn the heat to medium, and shake chicken to glaze evenly. Be careful as it can scorch easily. Let cool.

❹ Place rice in bento box and sprinkle with shredded *nori*. Slice chicken and place over the rice. Accompany with *beni-shoga*, or pickled ginger, if preferred.

menu

Eel *Teriyaki* Donburi
(see below)
Cheesy Spinach
(see p 66)
Kiwi Fruit
Agar-agar Jelly

Eel *Teriyaki Donburi*

Make thin omelet referring to page 14. Roll it and shred finely. In a frying pan, place 1 tsp rice wine or water and 2 oz (60 g) eel *teriyaki* (use vacuum packed or frozen type). Cover and heat until the liquid is gone. Pack rice in bento box and cover it with shredded omelet. Slice eel and arrange over the omelet.

Hint: Shredded omelet is very useful when you need vivid color. Freeze the remaining shreds in small portions to use for later.

EEL TERIYAKI BENTO

EGG FU YUNG BENTO

Egg Fu Yung

1 egg
1 oz (30 g) crabmeat
(fresh, canned or frozen)
1 Tbsp sliced green onion or scallion
1 *shiitake* mushroom, sliced
2 pea pods, sliced
1 tsp each rice vinegar, sugar and soy sauce
$2/3$ cup (4 oz /115 g) warm rice
2 tsp vegetable oil

1. In a small bowl, beat egg and combine with crabmeat and all the other ingredients except oil and rice.
2. Heat the oil in a small frying pan, and pour in the egg mixture all at once. Cook and stir over high heat, and shape into a thick disk. Turn over.
3. Pack rice in bento box, and cover it with Egg Fu Yung.

menu

Egg Fu Yung *Donburi* (see left)
Sautéed Lotus Root (see p 74)
Edamame (thaw frozen product)
Strawberries

23

SUSHI BENTO

As an all time favorite, sushi is everywhere now. They can make attractive bento and the variations are endless. Practice a few times, and you'll get the knack. As sushi rice contains vinegar which works as a preservative, it is also recommended for outings in warm weather.

menu
Sausage Rolls (see below)
Rolled Omelet (see p 61)
Bacon-wrapped Asparagus (see p 66)
Baby Apple Rabbits (see p 65)

Sausage Rolls

$2/3$ cup (4 oz /115g) sushi rice (see below)
$1/2$ sheet (4" x 8" /10 cm x 20 cm) *nori* seaweed
Filling: 2 cheese-stuffed sausages

Sushi Rice

1. In a small bowl, combine 1 Tbsp rice vinegar, $2/3$ Tbsp sugar and $1/3$ tsp salt.

2. Place steaming hot rice in a bowl, and pour the vinegar mixture over it. Mix with a slicing motion, separating rice grains. Let stand to cool.

Hint: Substitute sushi rice with plain rice, if preferred.

EASY SAUSAGE ROLL COMBO

How to make Sausage Roll
* This is an easy version using plastic wrap instead of traditional bamboo mat.

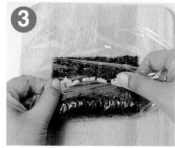

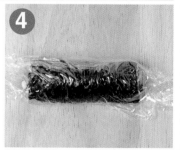

1 Lay $1/2$ sheet of *nori* over plastic wrap. For the best result, trim away top $1/5$ section ($1\frac{1}{2}$"/4 cm). Spread and lightly press sushi rice, leaving 1" (2.5 cm) at the top.

2 Place sausages stuffed with cheese in position. Regular or hot dog sausage can be used.

3 Lightly pressing the sausages with your fingers, bring up bottom side of wrap and start rolling carefully. Slightly wet the top edges to seal. Roll up and press with your hands.

4 Let stand until the *nori* is settled. Slice into the size of bento box height, without removing the wrap.

Nigiri-zushi Wrapped with *Nori*

²⁄₃ cup (4 oz /115 g) sushi rice (see p 24),
²⁄₃ sheet *nori* seaweed
Toppings: Salmon flakes, Boiled shrimp with mayonnaise (see below), Boiled baby sardines

Make sushi rice referring to previous page, and divide into quarter portions. Dip your hands in vinegared water, and make a tall, oval ball with one portion of rice by pressing with your fingers. Cut *nori* sheet into strips, slightly wider than the height of the rice, and long enough to overlap when wrapped around. Wrap this strip around the rice, creating a "cup" above the rice. Fill this "cup" with the topping.

> **Hint:** Try with toppings of your choice, such as scrambled egg, crabmeat, shredded carrots with raisins, cheese etc.

Boiled Shrimp with Mayonnaise

1 oz (30 g) boiled shrimp, 1 Tbsp mayonnaise, Dash soy sauce

Mix all ingredients.

menu
Nigiri-zushi Wrapped with **Nori** (see left)
Buttered Squash (see p 70)
Stuffed Fishcake (see p 73)
Sausage Sunflowers (see p 12, p 63)

NIGIRI-ZUSHI BENTO

KAMPYO-MAKI BENTO

Kampyo-maki

²⁄₃ cup (4 oz /115 g) sushi rice (see p 24)
¹⁄₄ sheet *nori* seaweed
Filling: Simmered *kampyo* (see below, or use commercial product)

Roll up referring to bottom of previous page, but placing the *nori* long side toward you (to make the roll thinner.) Cut to fit to the height of bento box. Add a mini bottle of soy sauce.

Simmered *Kampyo*

³⁄₈ oz (10 g) *kampyo*, 1 tsp salt, ³⁄₄ cup *dashi* stock, 2 Tbsp sugar, 2 Tbsp soy sauce

1. Wash *kampyo* and rub with ¹⁄₂ Tbsp of salt grains in a kneading motion until supple. Rinse off salt and boil in ample water until tender for 10 minutes.
2. In a saucepan, heat *dashi* stock, sugar and soy sauce to boiling. Add *kampyo* and simmer about 15 minutes until the sauce is absorbed. Cut into desired lengths, or fold at each side. (Makes 4 oz /115 g)

menu
Kampyo-maki (use commercial product or see below)
Mini Pork Cutlet (thaw frozen product)
Anpanman Potato (thaw frozen product)
Satsuma

> **Hint:** *Kampyo* makes a popular filling for many traditional sushi rolls to give a special texture and sweet and salty flavor. It is a long, dried strip shaved from a bottle-shaped gourd. Precooked *kampyo* is available at Japanese food stores.

menu
Flower Rolls (see below)
Sausage Octopus (see p 63)
Tomato, Cucumber and Cheese Skewers
(see p 69 and add cheese balls)
Orange Slices

Flower Rolls
1 cup (6 oz /170 g) sushi rice (see p 24)
³/₄ sheet *nori* seaweed
Fillings:
Pink *dembu* (fish flakes - see p 81)
Boiled spinach
Shredded omelet (see p 14 and shred finely)

FLOWER ROLL BENTO

How to make Flower Roll
* Fun rolls like this will tempt anti-vegetable children to eat.

1 Spread plastic wrap over a flat surface. Lay ½ sheet of *nori* on it, and place the sushi rice, leaving top 1" (2.5 cm) of *nori* uncovered. Form 3 "ridges" as shown.

2 In the "valleys," position spinach, fish flakes, shredded omelet and spinach in order.

3 Cover the center "ridge" with ¼ sheet of *nori*, and press lightly.

4 Carefully pressing the fillings inside, bring up near edges of plastic wrap and *nori* sheet so that it meets the top edge of rice. Roll up and press the whole roll, pushing in the rice on both sides. Slice with a wet knife.

Salad Rolls

1 cup (6 oz /170 g) sushi rice (see p 24), ½ sheet *nori* seaweed

Fillings: 1 Tbsp canned tuna, 3 seafood sticks, Shredded omelet (see p 14 and shred finely), Lettuce, Mayonnaise

1. Spread plastic wrap over a flat surface. Lay ½ sheet sheet of *nori* on it, and spread the sushi rice, leaving top 1" (2.5 cm) of *nori* uncovered. At about ⅓ to ½ from the bottom, place tuna, seafood sticks, shredded omelet, lettuce leaves and then mayonnaise, from side to side.

2. Carefully pressing the fillings inside, bring up near edges of plastic wrap and *nori* sheet so that it meets the top edge of rice. Roll up and press the whole roll, pushing in the rice on both sides.

3. Slice with a wet knife without removing the wrap.

menu

Salad Rolls (see left)
Chicken Nuggets (commercial)
Sweet Red Bean Skewers (commercial)
Strawberries

25

SALAD ROLL BENTO

Korean Rolls

1 cup (6 oz /170 g) sushi rice (see p 24), ½ sheet *nori*

Filling: Korean Salad (see p 75)

1. Spread plastic wrap over a flat surface. Lay ½ sheet sheet of *nori* on it, and spread the sushi rice, leaving top 1" (2.5 cm) of *nori* uncovered. At about ⅓ to ½ from the bottom, place Korean Salad over rice, from side to side.

2. Carefully pressing the fillings inside, bring up near edges of plastic wrap and *nori* sheet so that it meets the top edge of rice. Roll up and press the whole roll, pushing in the rice on both sides.

3. Slice with a wet knife without removing the wrap.

Korean Barbecue

2 oz (60 g) thinly sliced beef, 1 tsp soy sauce and *mirin*, garlic

1. In a small bowl, combine beef, soy sauce, *mirin* and grated garlic. Let stand 5-10 minutes.

2. In a heated frying pan, sauté marinated beef only briefly. Roll each piece with a lettuce leaf.

KOREAN ROLL BENTO

Hint: If substituting Korean seaweed with Japanese *nori*, brush on sesame oil, sprinkle with salt, and grill briefly until aroma is released.

menu

Korean Rolls (see left)
Korean Barbecue (see left)
Crab Stick Omelet (see p 61)
Agar-agar Jelly
Canned Satsuma

20

menu
Inari-zushi (see below)
Meatballs (see p 55)
Cod Roe and Jelly Noodles (see p 68)
Cooked Asparagus
 (Boil and sauté in butter)
Cherry tomatoes
Satsuma

Inari-zushi Pouches

2 *aburaage*, or thin fried *tofu* cakes for *Inari*, 1 cup water, 1 Tbsp soy sauce, 1 tsp each rice wine and sugar

Remove excess oil from *aburaage*, by pouring boiling water over them; drain. This process lets the seasoning penetrate into *aburaage*. Cut in half and open to make a pouch. In a saucepan heat water, soy sauce, sugar and rice wine to boiling. Add prepared aburaage. Cover and simmer 15 minutes until the sauce is almost gone. (Makes 4 *inari-zushi* pouches)

INARI-ZUSHI BENTO

Variation

Fold edges of pouch inside, and decorate top with pickled vegetables and fishcake.

How to make *Inari-zushi*

＊ Cook sushi rice referring to page 24, and use 1 cup (6 oz /170 g)

1 Combine sushi rice and 1 Tbsp toasted sesame seeds.

2 Divide the mixed sushi rice into two portions, and make 2 oval shaped rice balls.

3 Lightly squeeze out extra sauce from the pouches. Open them and pack the rice ball into each.

4 Close the opening by layering the edges. Press the whole sushi to settle.

Natto Rice Balls

1 Tbsp *natto* (fermented soy beans), $^2/_3$ cup (4 oz /115 g) sushi rice (see p 24), 3 $^1/_4$ sheets *nori* seaweed

Spread $^1/_3$ portion of sushi rice over the *nori*. Place 1 tsp *natto* mixed with a dash of soy sauce. Carefully wrap up with *nori*, lightly pressing the rice to stick together, but do not push out the filling.

Hint: Try healthy *natto* this way as it is much tastier when used as a sushi filling.

menu

Natto Rice Balls (see left)
Potato Rolls (see p 74)
String Beans with Sesame Dressing (see p 66)
Cherry Tomatoes
Kiwi Fruit Slice
Persimmon Wedges

NATTO ONIGIRI BENTO

SUSHI DOLL BENTO

menu

Sushi Dolls (see below)
Easy Mixed *Tempura* (see p 68)
Spinach with Black Sesame Dressing (see p 66)
Cherry Tomatoes
Jellied Satsuma (see page 77)

Sushi Dolls

1 beaten egg, $^2/_3$ cup (4 oz /115 g) sushi rice (see p 24), 2-3 Tbsp *chirashi-zushi* mix (commercial - see p 81) or 1 Tbsp toasted sesame seeds

Make 2 thin omelets referring to page 14. Combine sushi rice and *chirashi-zushi* mix (or toasted sesame seeds.) Divide the mixed rice in half, and make two round rice balls. Referring to page 14, wrap the rice ball with the omelet, and loosely bind the top with a stem of boiled spinach. Open out and trim omelet edges to resemble flower petals, if possible. Attach black sesame seed eyes to a cheese ball, and set with a party pick.

menu

Temari-zushi (see below)
Kamaboko Rabbits (see p 63)
Stewed Celery (see p 67)
Cheesy Spinach (see p 66)
Sweet Potato Dumpling (see p 70)

Temari-zushi
$^2/_3$ cup (4 oz /115 g) cooked rice, 2-3 Tbsp *chirashi-zushi* mix (commercial), Thin omelet (see p 14), String beans, Pink *dembu* (fish flakes - see p 81)

Hint: *Temari-zushi,* or decorated sushi ball, originated in Kyoto. It is very easy to make and eat. Design a pattern of your own.

TEMARI-ZUSHI BENTO

How to make *Temari-zushi*

In a small bowl combine warm rice and *chirashi-zushi* mix. Divide into two and shape into round balls.

Make flower shapes from thin omelet. Slice cooked string bean diagonally. Arrange them in the center of plastic wrap.

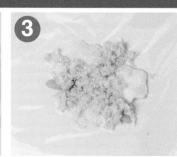

Fill the gaps with pink *dembu* to show the contrast.

Position the sushi ball on it, and wrap up pressing lightly to let the toppings settle.

Sushi Cake

²/₃ cup (4 oz /115 g) sushi rice (see p 24), ¹/₂ boiled egg, minced, 1 Tbsp Beef *Soboro* (see p 60)
Toppings: *Kamaboko* (fishcake - see p 81), Pink *dembu* (fish flakes - see p 81), carrot shapes, cherry

1. Divide sushi rice into two portions. Mix well one portion with minced boiled egg, and the other with Beef *Soboro*. Lay plastic wrap over a round mold, and place pink *dembu* on the bottom. Place egg and rice mixture, and flatten the surface with a spoon. Layer with Beef *Soboro* mixture.
2. Unmold and turn over. Decorate with favorite food slices. Here, fish products and cut-out carrots are used.

Hint: This will make a surprise bento for birthdays and anniversaries.

menu
Sushi Cake (see left)
Fried Siu Mai Dumplings
 (simply deep-fry commercial dumplings)
Apple Leaves (see p 65)
Grapes

SUSHI CAKE

SUSHI SALAD BENTO

menu
Sushi Salad (see below)
Fried Chicken (see p 56)
Cherry Tomatoes
Agar-agar Jelly
Dried Tuna Cubes

Sushi Salad

²/₃ cup (4 oz /115 g) hot rice, 2 tsp sushi vinegar or favorite vinegar dressing, Lettuce
Toppings: Sliced ham, cheese, carrot and cucumber, shaped with a cutter

In a small bowl combine hot rice and vinegar dressing, and let stand to cool. Place sushi rice in a container, and arrange toppings in your favorite pattern.

Hint: Be sure to use steaming hot rice for sushi. Cold rice does not absorb vinegar mixture and results in soggy sushi rice.

BREAD BENTO

Make these appetizing petite sandwiches for little fingers instead of the same old PB & J. Try to create traditional sandwiches with these new twists.

menu

"Look at Me" Animal Sandwiches
(see below)
Chicken Nuggets (commercial)
Cherry Tomatoes
Agar-agar Jelly

"Look at Me" Animal Sandwiches
Layer 2 slices of sandwich bread, and slice into quarters. Using cookie cutters, cut out shapes from 4 pieces only. Spread butter over one side of each slice, and place filling. Add sesame seed eyes and/ or mouth.

"LOOK AT ME" ANIMAL SANDWICH BENTO

Filling Ideas

Chopped Boiled Egg Mixed with Mayonnaise

Ham

Blueberry Jam

Orange Marmalade

menu
Pocket Sandwiches (see below)
Tofu **Dumplings** (see p 77)
Strawberry
Kiwi Fruit

Pocket Sandwiches

1 ³/₄ " (2 cm) thick slice white bread
Pork cutlet (leftover or frozen)
Tonkatsu sauce
 (thick Worcestershire sauce)
Finely shredded cabbage

Cut bread in half. Make a deep slit into the cut edge. Pour generous amount of *tonkatsu* sauce over the cutlet and shredded cabbage and fill in the pocket.

Hint: Pocket sandwiches are perfect for sauced fillings as they are leak proof.

POCKET SANDWICH BENTO

ROLLED SANDWICH BENTO

menu
Rolled Sandwiches (see below)
Cole Slaw (see p 67)
Curried Quail Eggs and Cucumber Skewers
 (see p 71 for Curried Quail Eggs)
Strawberries

Rolled Sandwiches

3 slices sandwich bread
Fillings: Ham, *nori* and sliced cheese Taramo Salad (see p 69)

Over a piece of plastic wrap, lay a slice of buttered bread. Place a slice of ham over it, and roll up. Twist side edges of the wrap to close. Slice through the plastic wrap and pack into a container.

Hint: The filling should reach the end of the bread so it won't come apart. The plastic wrap will keep the bread moist. Choose fillings that won't leak during storage.

33

menu

Yakisoba Roll (see below)
German Potatoes (see p 72)
Cheesy Spinach (see p 66)
Milk Jelly (see p 76)

Yakisoba Roll
See page 44 for *Yakisoba*.
Since *Yakisoba* Rolls are high in
carbohydrates, include a good amount of
vegetables to make a balanced meal.

YAKISOBA ROLL BENTO

How to make *Yakisoba* Roll

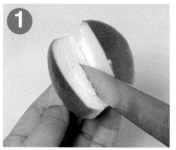

1

Slit a bread roll. Using a
sharp knife, make a deep
score.

2

Hollow out both sides.

3

Spread butter inside to
prevent the bread from
getting wet. Toast briefly
and fill with a generous
amount of *yakisoba*.

Bread Cup

Variation
Slice off top section of the
roll. Scoop out inside to
make a hollow.

menu

Mini Hamburgers (see below)
Butter Potato Dumpling (see p 73)
Carrot Salad (see p 68)
Jellied Mangoes (see p 77)

Mini Hamburgers (see p 54)

2 small hamburger patties,
2 bread rolls or mini buns,
Lettuce, Yellow bell pepper
slices, Pickle slices, Ketchup

Slit deeply into bread rolls or
buns. Lightly spread butter
inside. Sandwich lettuce,
hamburger, dab of ketchup,
pepper slices, pickles, and/or
choice of garnishes: sliced
tomato, onion, bacon, and
avocado, with mayonnaise.
Secure the sandwich with a
food pick.

Hint: Smaller sized
hamburgers will not slip
out when held in small
hands.

MINI HAMBURGER BENTO

MINI HOT DOG BENTO

menu

Mini Hot Dogs (see below)
Tomato, Cucumber and Cheese Skewers
(see p 69 and add cheese balls)
Baked Sweet Potatoes (see p 76)
Grapes

Mini Hot Dogs

2 bread rolls
2 wiener sausages
Lettuce
Ketchup

Slit into bread rolls along the
center. Lightly spread butter
inside. Shred washed and
dried lettuce. Fill the roll with
shredded lettuce and sausage,
and choice of garnishes.

Hint: Add a mini bottle of
ketchup and/or mustard so
the eater can personalize
his or her lunch.

Rolled Pancakes
2 oz (60g) pancake mix,
1/3 cup water or buttermilk
Filling: 2 Tbsp Potato Salad (see p 72),
2 wiener sausages, Lettuce

ROLLED PANCAKE BENTO

How to make Pancakes

1 Combine pancake mix and water (or milk) until smooth.

2 In a heated non-stick frying pan, pour in half of the pancake batter.

3 Reduce heat to low, and cook until the surface is bubbly. Turn over and cook briefly.

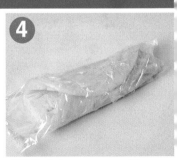

4 While hot, wrap up with plastic wrap, and let cool to set. Make 2 and fill one with sausages and lettuce, and the other with potato salad.

Teddy Pancakes

2 oz (60g) pancake mix
$^1/_2$ beaten egg
3 Tbsp milk
Chocolate sauce

Combine pancake mix, beaten egg and milk just to combine. Pour into heated non-stick frying pan. Make a cake large enough to cut out 3 teddy faces. Turn over and cook until done. Let cool before using cookie cutter. Using chocolate sauce, draw bear's faces. If tube type paste is not available, roll up the sauce in plastic wrap and make a tiny hole to squeeze out.

Hint: For clear edges, place the pancake right side (face) down, and then cut out with a cookie cutter.

menu
Teddy Pancakes (see left)
Chicken Nuggets (commercial)
Glazed Mini Carrots (see p 68)
Orange Slices
Kiwi Fruit Slices

TEDDY PANCAKE BENTO

VEGGIE PANCAKE BENTO

menu
Veggie Pancakes (see below)
Boiled Egg (sprinkle *goma-shio* (sesame seed salt) over halves)
Quick Cooked Apples (see p 77)
Grapes

Veggie Pancakes

2 oz (60g) pancake mix
$^1/_2$ beaten egg
2 Tbsp frozen vegetable mix

Combine pancake mix, beaten egg, milk and vegetable mix just to combine. Pour half portion of the batter into heated non-stick frying pan. When the surface becomes bubbly, turn over and cook until done. Cut into bite-size pieces before packing.

37

menu

French Toast (see below)
Sausage Pineapples (see p 20)
Anpanman Potatoes (frozen)
Apple Rabbit (see p 20)

FRENCH TOAST BENTO

How to make French Toast

2 slices baguette
1 egg
¹⁄₂ cup milk
2 tsp sugar
¹⁄₂ Tbsp butter

1 Make egg mixture by combining egg, milk and sugar.

2 Slice baguette into bite-size pieces, and soak in the egg mixture. Use a plastic bag for ease.

3 Melt butter in a frying pan, and cook both sides until partially browned. Let cool to pack.

Croque-Monsieur

2 ½"(1.5 cm) thick slices bread
2 slices each ham and cheese

Butter the inside of sandwich grill. Place ham and a cheese between bread slices, and cook both sides until golden. Let cool and cut into quarters.
If using a frying pan, melt butter and place a slice of bread, then layer ham, cheese and another slice of bread. Cook over low heat, pressing the sandwich. Turn over.

> **Hint:** When cooking broccoli, add a few drops of vegetable oil and a pinch of salt to boiling water before adding broccoli florets, and cook only briefly. This way a fresh green color is obtained.

menu
Croque-Monsieur (see left)
Boiled Broccoli
Candied Sweet Potatoes
 (see p 76)

CROQUE-MONSIEUR BENTO

TACO SANDWICH BENTO

Taco Sandwiches

2 thin slices of bread
3 oz (85 g) ground beef
1½ oz (40 g) each
 minced onion and carrot
5 cherry tomatoes, minced
1 Tbsp taco seasoning
Shredded cheese
Lettuce, washed and shredded
1 tsp vegetable oil

Heat vegetable oil in a frying pan, and cook minced onion, carrot and tomatoes briefly. Add ground beef and stir-fry until heated through. Add taco seasoning and ¼ cup water, and continue to cook over low heat, until the liquid is gone. Butter one side of sliced bread, and place cheese, taco meat and lettuce. Fold the bread in half, and wrap tightly with plastic wrap.

menu
Taco Sandwiches (see left)
Tomato and Cucumber Skewers
 (see p 69)
Potato Chips
Satsuma

39

PASTA BENTO

In any region of the world, pastas are always a favorite, especially of children. The smooth and slippery texture cooked and seasoned in various ways has pleased palates for years. By combining pasta with a variety of foods, you can make a nutritiously balanced bento.

menu
Spaghetti "Napolitan"
 (see below)
Chicken Nuggets
 (commercial)
Potato Salad (see p 72)
Grapes
Cherry Tomato

Hint: If the eater can only hold a spoon, use macaroni in place of spaghetti, or just break spaghetti into two or three pieces.

SPAGHETTI "NAPOLITAN" BENTO

How to make Spaghetti "Napolitan"

1½ - 2 oz (40-60 g) spaghetti
1 oz (30 g) each minced
carrot and onion
½ bell pepper, thinly sliced
2 strips bacon, sliced
2 Tbsp ketchup
1 tsp butter

Heat ample water to boil, and add a generous pinch of salt. Cook spaghetti according to the time suggested on the package. Meanwhile melt butter in a frying pan and sauté bacon and vegetables until supple. Add drained spaghetti and ketchup to the pan, and mix well until the liquid is gone.

Spaghetti Bolognese

1½-2 oz (40-60 g) spaghetti, 1½ oz (40 g) ground beef, 1 Tbsp each minced onion and carrot, 2 Tbsp canned tomato, 3 Tbsp ketchup, 3 Tbsp Worcestershire sauce, 1 tsp butter, 1 tsp olive oil, Sliced cheese

Heat ample water to boil, and add a generous pinch of salt. Cook spaghetti according to the time suggested on the package. Meanwhile combine all the ingredients except spaghetti and sliced cheese in a microwave safe container. Cover and microwave 3 minutes at 500 W. Take out from the oven, and stir well. Microwave a further 30 seconds, uncovered to release excess moisture. Drain cooked spaghetti and toss with olive oil. Place it in bento box, and pour in Bolognese sauce over it. Top with cut-out slices of cheese.

menu

Spaghetti Bolognese (see left)
Potato Croquette (frozen)
Jellied Tangerine (see p 77)
Strawberries

SPAGHETTI BOLOGNESE BENTO

SPAGHETTI WITH MUSHROOMS BENTO

Spaghetti with Mushrooms

1½-2 oz (40-60 g) spaghetti, 2 strips bacon, 1½ oz (40 g) mixed mushrooms (*shiitake*, *maitake*, *eryingii*), 1 tsp butter, ½ Tbsp soy sauce or oyster sauce, Dash salt

Heat ample water to boil, and add a generous pinch of salt. Cook spaghetti according to the time suggested on the package. Meanwhile slice bacon and mushrooms into bite-size pieces. Melt butter in a frying pan, and sauté bacon and mushroom pieces. Drain cooked spaghetti and transfer into the frying pan. Mix and season with salt and soy (or oyster) sauce.

Hint: The more variety of mushrooms added, the more tasty the pasta will be as you can enjoy different textures and flavors.

menu

Spaghetti with Mushrooms (see left)
Crab Stick Omelet (see p 61)
Sweet Red Bean Skewers (commercial)
Cherry Tomato and Cucumber Skewers
Strawberry

41

menu
Somen **Noodles** (see below)
Sui Mai Dumplings (see below)
Apple Tulips (see p 65)

Somen Noodles

1 bundle (1³/₄ oz/ 50 g) dried *somen*
¹/₂ cup (120 ml) *soba/udon* dipping sauce (straight type)

Sui Mai Dumplings

Referring to page 55, make meatball mixture, and wrap one portion with a commercial sui mai wrapper. Make 3. On a microwave safe plate, lay a cabbage leaf to prevent sticking, and arrange sui mai dumplings on it. Microwave 1 minute and 30 seconds at 500W or until cooked.

SOMEN NOODLE BENTO

How to make *Somen* Noodle Bento

* *Somen* is Japanese fine wheat noodles.

1 In ample boiling water, cook 1³/₄ oz (50 g) *somen* noodles 1-2 minutes or as directed on the package. Blanch in cold water and drain in a colander. Immediately wind some *somen* around your fingers.

2 Arrange *somen* swirls in a bento box. This way the noodles don't get tangled when picked up. Arrange toppings of cut-out cucumber and thin omelet slices. Center cherry tomato.

Be sure to accompany with dipping sauce. Fill sauce container with straight or diluted *soba/udon* sauce. Larger containers are to be used as a dipping cup, and the smaller ones for pouring over.

Yaki Udon Noodles

1³⁄₄ oz (50 g) dried *udon*,
¹⁄₄ onion, sliced, 1" (2.5 cm)
carrot, shredded, 1 large
cabbage leaf, sliced, ¹⁄₂
Tbsp concentrated *soba/
udon* dipping sauce (straight type),
naruto(fishcake - see p 81)
slices, 1 tsp vegetable oil

In ample boiling water, cook
udon noodles as suggested on
the package. Meanwhile, heat
vegetable oil in a frying pan,
and stir-fry carrot, onion and
cabbage leaf. Add drained
udon, and drizzle in *soba/udon*
dipping sauce diluted with
2 Tbsp water. Cook and stir
constantly until the liquid is gone.
Garnish with *naruto* slices.

> **Hint:** Enhance the flavor
> of fried noodles with
> dried bonito shavings sold
> in packets. Accompany
> the noodles with topping.
> (They get soggy if
> sprinkled beforehand)

YAKI UDON BENTO

menu
Yaki Udon Noodles (see left)
Sausage Pineapples (see p 20)
Jellied Mango (see p 77)
Cherry Tomatoes

HIYASHI KITSUNE UDON BENTO

Hiyashi Kitsune Udon Noodles

1³⁄₄ oz (50 g) dried *udon*
2 *Inari-zushi* Pouches (see p 28)
Lettuce
Carrot
Soba/udon dipping sauce
(*straight type*)

In ample boiling water, cook
udon noodles as suggested on
the package. Slice *inari-zushi*
pouches referring to page 28
(or use leftover pouches) into
wide strips. Tear or shred
lettuce leaves. Shred carrot.
Place drained *udon* in bento
box, and top with lettuce,
carrot and *inari-zushi* pouches.
Accompany with a bottle
of *soba/udon* sauce (dilute
according to the package) to
pour over.

> **Hint:** Try sesame sauce
> (*gomadare*, sold in a bottle)
> for richer flavor.

menu
Hiyashi Kitsune Udon Noodles (see left)
Fried Chicken (see p 56)
Boiled Broccoli
Orange Slices

43

Yakisoba Noodles

½ portion precooked *yakisoba* or Chinese noodles (commercial),
1 oz (30 g) thin slices of pork loin, cut up,
1 large cabbage leaf, shredded, ¼ onion, sliced,
2" (5 cm) carrot, shredded, ½ bell pepper, sliced,
2 Tbsp *yakisoba* or *tonkatsu* sauce (thick Worcestershire sauce
– commercially available as Bulldog Sauce),
1 tsp vegetable oil, *aonori* (green laver), optional

Heat vegetable oil in a frying pan, and stir-fry sliced meat and vegetables just until supple. Add half portion precooked noodles and 3 Tbsp water. Keep stirring to separate the noodles. Add *yakisoba* sauce, and stir-fry until there is no moisture. Place in bento box and sprinkle *aonori*, if preferred.

YAKISOBA NOODLE BENTO

Handling Precooked Noodles	**Salt *Yakisoba***	***Yakisoba* Omelet**

For ease of eating, cut precooked noodles, cut into halves or quarters after removing from the bag.	Use *dashi* granules and salt in place of the sweet, thick *yakisoba* or *tonkatsu* sauce, and place toppings of your choice: sliced *chikuwa* (tubular fishcake - see p 81), ham and vegetables.	Make a thin omelet referring to page 18, and wrap *yakisoba* with it for added volume.

Fried Rice Noodles

1 oz (30 g) dried rice noodles
2 strips bacon, 5-6 shrimp
(fresh or frozen), 2" (5 cm)
carrot, ½ bell pepper, ⅙ onion,
½ tsp chicken stock granules,
Dash oyster sauce and sesame oil,
½ tsp vegetable oil

Soak rice noodles in water until
soft. Slice bacon and vegetables.
Shell and devein shrimp. Heat
lightly greased frying pan
and sauté bacon, and then
add sliced vegetables. Lastly
add shrimp. When shrimp
are cooked, add softened rice
noodles. Stir-fry, separating
noodles, and sprinkle with
chicken stock granules and a
dash of oyster sauce. Drizzle
sesame oil along the edges of
the pan and remove from heat.

> **Hint:** If using instant rice
> noodles which are already
> seasoned, no soaking is
> necessary. Just add water
> to the noodles and let
> steam in the pan.

menu

Fried Rice Noodles (see left)
Tomato and Cucumber Skewers (see p 69)
Fried Sesame Dumpling (see p76)
Jellied Satsuma (see p77)

FRIED RICE NOODLE BENTO

SEAFOOD FRIED NOODLE BENTO

Seafood Fried Noodles

½ portion precooked *yakisoba*
noodles (commercial), 1 oz (30
g) frozen mixed seafood,
1 *shiitake* mushroom, ½ oz (15g)
bamboo shoot, ½ cabbage
leaf, 2"(5 cm) carrot, ½ bell
pepper, 1 tsp chicken stock
granules, Dash salt, 1 tsp each
cornstarch and vegetable oil

In a heated frying pan, stir-fry
precooked noodles, sprinkling
with water to separate the
noodles. (Commercial *yakisoba*
noodles are already greased
and need no oil) Let cool, and
place in bento box. Heat the
pan and add vegetable oil. Stir-
fry thawed mixed seafood over
high heat. Add chicken stock
granules and salt to taste.
Dissolve cornstarch with an
equal amount of water, and
drizzle over, stirring for even
thickening. Pour over the
noodles.

> **Hint:** Separate noodles
> and topping, if preferred

menu

Seafood Fried Noodles (see left)
Almond (see p 77)

BENTO FOR WARM WEATHER

It is wise to avoid raw or perishable food during hot summer weather. Take advantage of frozen foods and use them as "food preservatives" to keep the bento cool until lunchtime. *Umeboshi*, or pickled Japanese plums, have been used as natural preservatives in bento as well as a popular rice companion for their refreshing, sour flavor. Also, fried foods keep well on summer outings since they have been cooked in high temperature oil.

menu
Curry & Rice Croquettes (see below)
Mini Quiche (see p 71)
Sautéed Red Bell Pepper (see p 69)
Petit Cucumber Salad (see below)

Curry & Rice Croquettes
²/₃ cup (4 oz /115 g) warm rice
3 Tbsp meat and vegetable curry
All purpose flour
Beaten egg
Breadcrumbs
Vegetable oil for deep frying

Petit Cucumber Salad
Slice cucumber into about ¹/₄" (5-6 mm) thicknesses, and cut out a shape using a cookie cutter. Toss with dash French dressing.

Quick Curry

Sauté diced meat or chicken with cubed vegetables such as carrot, onion, potato, celery and mushroom. Add water to cover and simmer until fork-tender. Dissolve 2 cakes (1 oz /30 g) or 1 portion of Japanese curry roux per cup, and simmer 10 minutes.

CURRY & RICE CROQUETTE COMBO

How to make Curry & Rice Croquettes

1 In a bowl, combine curry and warm rice well. Use leftover curry.

2 Using plastic wrap, make 2 rice balls.

3 While still warm, coat with flour, beaten egg, and then with breadcrumbs.

4 Deep-fry in oil on medium heat, until crisp. Drain oil and let stand to cool.

Mixed *Tempura Donburi*

1 oz (30 g) shelled shrimp
Some *mitsuba*, or trefoil
Tempura flour
Tsuyu no moto

Devein shrimp and pat dry. Cut up *mitsuba*. Make *tempura* batter by combining the same amount of *tempura* flour and cold water in a bowl, and add shrimp and *mitsuba*. Mix until they are just coated, and take a bite-size portion in a spoon and slide into oil preheated to medium. When the *tempura* floats to the surface of the oil and bubbles get smaller, take out and drain. Dip in *tsuyu no moto*, diluted if necessary, and place over rice.

> **Hint:** Mix vegetables with children's favorites such as sausage or potatoes.

menu

Mixed *Tempura Donburi* (see left)
Chikuzen-ni (Braised Chicken and Vegetables) (see p 75)
***Edamame*, or young soy beans** (frozen)
Cherry Tomato
Cheese Balls (commercial)

MIXED TEMPURA COMBO

PLUM BLOSSOM RICE COMBO

menu

Plum Blossom Rice (see below)
Squash Balls (see p 75)
Asparagus and Sausage Skewers (see below)
Cherry Tomato
Agar-agar Jelly
Canned Satsuma

Plum Blossom Rice

²/₃ cup (4 oz /115 g) warm rice
Shiso furikake (rice sprinkles - see p 81)
Crispy small pickled plums

Mix rice with sprinkles and place in bento box. Cut crispy plums into halves, remove stones, and arrange on the rice to resemble a plum blossom.

Asparagus and Sausage Skewers

Choose asparagus as thick as sausage, and cut to the same size. Sauté them in a greased frying pan, and season with salt and pepper. Using a food pick, skewer alternately.

47

menu
Toasted *Onigiri* (frozen, or see below)
Fried Squid Rings (frozen, or see below)
Macaroni Gratin (frozen, or see p 50)
Candied Sweet Potatoes (frozen, or see p 76)
Satsuma

TOASTED ONIGIRI COMBO

Toasted *Onigiri*

In a bowl, combine ²/₃ cup (4 oz /115 g) warm rice and 2 tsp soy sauce.
Make a triangular *onigiri* (see bottom of page 8). In a non-stick frying pan,
cook both sides on low heat until the surface is crisp.

Fried Squid Rings

Slice squid and dry with paper towel. Sprinkle with dash salt and pepper.
Refer to page 57 for coating, and deep-fry until golden.

Advice

Commercial frozen foods are
ideal for the warm season.
Some frozen products are
made to be thawed naturally
by lunch time.

menu
Carrot Rice Omelet (see below)
Fried Sui Mai Dumplings (frozen)
Edamame, or young soy beans (frozen)
Agar-agar Jelly

Carrot Rice Omelet
²/₃ cup (4 oz /115 g) warm rice,
1 oz (30 g) carrot, minced,
1 Tbsp ketchup, 1 tsp butter,
Dash salt

In a microwave safe container,
put minced carrot and butter.
Cover and microwave 1 minute.
Add rice and mix well. Add
ketchup and a dash of salt while
hot. Wrap in omelet referring
to page 18.
Place omelet in bento box, and
make a crisscross incision on
top. Accompany a mini bottle
of ketchup.
Deep-fry sui mai dumplings, and
let cool. Pack frozen *edamame*
(thawing is not necessary)

Hint: In warm weather,
it is wise to freeze agar-
agar jelly as it will keep the
bento cool.

CARROT RICE OMELET COMBO

JAPANESE RED BEAN RICE COMBO

Japanese Red Rice (*Sekihan*)
3 cups glutinous rice, ¹/₂ cup dried adzuki
beans, Toasted sesame seeds, Dash salt

Rinse and soak glutinous rice in water about
30 minutes. Meanwhile in a saucepan heat
to boiling dried adzuki beans in water to
cover. Discard boiling water, and add water
again. Cook about 10 minutes and transfer
into a colander, saving the cooking water
this time. Drain soaked rice, and place in
a rice cooker. Dilute the saved water to 3
cups, and add to the cooker. Turn on the
cooker.
(Makes 6 portions)

Note:
Sekihan, or red rice, is a Japanese
traditional staple for special occasions.
To celebrate family events, people would
give away a box of *sekihan* to each of
their neighbors and share the joy.

Lotus Root Sandwich *Tempura*
1" (2.5 cm) lotus root, Cornstarch for
dusting, 1 oz (30 g) ground pork or chicken,
1 Tbsp minced green onion, Dash salt, ¹/₂
cup all-purpose flour, Green laver (optional)

Peel lotus root and slice into ¹/₄" (5-6 mm)
thick rounds. Blanch in water, drain and
dust with cornstarch. Combine ground pork
or chicken, green onion and salt. Sandwich
half of this mixture with lotus slices. Make
batter with all purpose flour and same
amount of water (Add *aonori* /green laver,
if preferred). Dip sandwich in batter, and
deep-fry in medium hot oil until crisp. Cut
into bite size pieces.

Strawberry Bavarian Cream
Refer to Milk Jelly on page 76, substituting
milk with sweet condensed milk. Top with
strawberry jam.

menu
Japanese Red Rice (*Sekihan*, see left)
Fried Lotus Root Sandwich *Tempura* (see left)
String Beans with Sesame Dressing (see p 66)
Strawberry Bavarian Cream (see left)

BENTO FOR COLD WEATHER

If the bento can be reheated at lunchtime, the children will feel the warmth from home.
An alumite bento box is worth investing in for this purpose. Place on a warm heater until lunch time.
These bento are rich in flavor and very filling.

menu
Macaroni Gratin (see below)
Strawberries and Banana with Custard
(see p 77 for Quick Custard Sauce)

MACARONI GRATIN BENTO

Macaroni Gratin
$^2/_3$ oz (20 g) macaroni, $^1/_4$ onion,
$^2/_3$ oz (20 g) shelled shrimp,
2 strips bacon, 2 broccoli florets,
$^1/_2$ Tbsp grated cheese, 1 tsp vegetable oil
White sauce: $^1/_2$ cup milk, 2 Tbsp all-purpose flour,
 1 Tbsp butter, Bouillon granules, Salt and pepper

Cook macaroni in ample boiling water with a pinch of salt. Add broccoli to cook 1 minute before draining the macaroni. In a frying pan, sauté chopped onion, sliced bacon and shrimp. Add them and cooked macaroni to the white sauce (see below), and mix well. Butter the inside of bento box, and pour the macaroni mixture in. Sprinkle with grated cheese, and bake 10 minutes in toaster oven.

Quick White Sauce

1

Pour milk in microwave safe bowl. Add flour through a sieve. Cover with plastic wrap, and microwave 3 minutes at 500W.

2

Remove wrap and stir vigorously using a whisk.

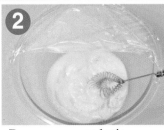

3

Add the remaining white sauce ingredients, and stir again.

4

Cover with plastic wrap again, and microwave 2 minutes. Immediately remove from oven, and stir quickly to make a smooth sauce.

menu
Curry & Rice (see below)
***Wakame* and Cucumber with Vinegar**
 (see p 66)
Cherry Tomato

Curry & Rice

Use leftover curry from the day before, by reheating it. (To make quick curry, see page 46) Place $\frac{1}{3}$ cup (2 oz/ 60 g) warm rice in bento box, and pour a portion of curry over it. Cover with $\frac{1}{3}$ cup rice. Arrange a slice of cooked ham, curried quail eggs and a sausage to resemble a Martian or robot face.

Hint: This way the runny curry sauce is not supposed to leak, but avoid swinging the box on the way.

CURRY & RICE BENTO

TEMPURA AND EGG DONBURI BENTO

Tempura and Egg *Donburi*

Chikuwa (tubular fishcake - see p 81) *Tempura* (frozen), Squid *Tempura* (frozen), $\frac{1}{3}$ onion, sliced, $\frac{1}{3}$ cup *Soba/udon* dipping sauce (straight type), 1 beaten egg

In a saucepan, heat *Tsuyu no moto* and onion. When onion slices are transparent, add *tempura* cut into bite-size pieces and cook until heated through. Pour over beaten egg just until set. Lay over rice packed in bento box.

Hint: Try with any frozen or leftover *tempura*. When making *donburi*, or rice with juicy toppings, pack side dish and dessert in a different container.

menu
Tempura* and Egg *Donburi
 (see left)
***Nori*-wrapped *Hampen* and Cheese**
 (see p 74)
Cherry Tomato

Hint: This is a good way of using leftover pork or chicken cutlet or fried shrimp. The sweet and salty sauce will turn a leftover cutlet into a delicacy.

menu

Katsudon, or saucy pork cutlet on rice
 (see below)
Wakame and Sardines (see p 75)
Baby Apple Rabbits (see p 65)

KATSUDON BENTO

How to make *Katsudon*

Katsudon

²/₃ cup (4 oz /115 g) warm rice
¹/₄ onion, sliced
¹/₂-²/₃ pork cutlet
1 egg, lightly beaten
Cooked sweet peas
Cooking sauce:
1 Tbsp soy sauce
1 tsp each sugar and *mirin*
3 Tbsp reconstituted
 dashi stock

Heat cooking sauce ingredients to boiling. Add sliced onion.

Then add pork cutlet sliced into ¹/₂" (1.5 cm) widths, and cook over medium-low heat until the sauce is absorbed.

Pour beaten egg over ingredients in the pan, and shake the pan to fluff. Cover and cook over low heat just until the egg is set. Place warm rice in bento box, and arrange topping.

Chinese *Donburi*

²/₃ cup (4 oz /115 g) warm rice, ¹/₂ oz (15 g) thinly sliced pork, ²/₃ oz (20 g) frozen mixed seafood, 1-2 ear fungi, or black mushroom, ¹/₂ oz (15 g) each onion, carrot, bamboo shoot, ¹/₃ Chinese cabbage leaf, 2 pea pods, ¹/₂ tsp chicken stock granules, Dash salt, oyster sauce, soy sauce and sesame oil, 1 tsp cornstarch, ¹/₂ tsp vegetable oil

Cut vegetables and mushroom into random pieces. Place rice in bento box. Heat a frying pan, grease, and stir-fry pork and frozen seafood until heated through. Add vegetables and mushroom, and cook over high heat. Stir in seasonings and drizzle sesame oil along the edges of the pan. Dissolve cornstarch with same amount of water, and stir in to thicken the sauce. Pour over rice.

menu
**Chinese *Donburi*
 or Chinese Rice Bowl** (see left)
Almond Tofu (see p 77)

CHINESE DONBURI BENTO

CHINESE PORK BUN BENTO

menu
Steamed Pork Bun (see below)
Egg Fu Yung (see p 23)
Boiled Broccoli
Strawberries

Steamed Pork Bun

Steam the frozen pork bun as directed on the package. To prevent the bottom of bun from drying, line metal container with a cabbage leaf. It will keep the bun moist.

ALL TIME FAVORITES

Hamburgers, fried chicken, rolled omelet and fried prawns are always welcomed by the young. They are the foods that keep the tastes and textures even when cooled after a period of time. Be creative with such staple dishes and add a little ingenuity so as to supply a variety of foodstuff and nutrition.

menu

Mini Hamburgers (see below)
Molded *Onigiri* (see p 12)
Macaroni Salad (see p 72)
Boiled Broccoli
Cherry Tomato
Strawberry
Cheese Cupcake (see p 76)

> **Mini Hamburgers**
> 12 oz (340 g) ground beef,
> ¹/₂ onion, chopped, ¹/₂ carrot, chopped,
> ¹/₂ cup breadcrumbs, ¹/₄ cup milk,
> 1 egg, ¹/₂ tsp salt, Dash pepper
> (Makes 6 to dozen)

HAMBURGER COMBO

How to make Mini Hamburgers

1 Microwave chopped onion spread on a plate and covered, for 2 minutes at 500W. Soak breadcrumbs in milk until softened. Place all ingredients in a bowl.

2 Combine well. Add salt and pepper. Mix well in a kneading motion until sticky.

3 Divide into 6 patties, each about 3 Tbsp. Cook in non-stick frying pan right away.

4 For later uses, arrange on a metal tray and put in a freezer. After 2 to 3 hours, take out and pack in freezer bag for later use.

5 This portion will make a dozen meatballs or patties of about 1¹/₂ Tbsp size. Make remainder into balls for a change. See next page for Chinese meatballs.

menu

Mini Scotch Eggs (see below)
Triangular *Onigiri* (see p 8)
Sautéed Greens (see p 66)
Apple Sweet Potatoes (see p 70)

Mini Scotch Eggs

1 portion Mini Hamburger
 (see previous page)
2 boiled quail eggs (available in can)
Ketchup
Worcestershire sauce

Coat quail eggs with flour. Halve
1 portion Mini Hamburger
patty, and wrap a quail egg
with the half patty. Make 2 and
cook in a greased frying pan,
rolling occasionally until heated
through. Heat the equal amount
of ketchup and Worcestershire
sauce in a saucepan, and add
Scotch eggs. Cook until the
Scotch eggs are coated with
thickened sauce.

MINI SCOTCH EGG BENTO

MEATBALL BENTO

Glazed Meatballs

2 oz (60 g) ground pork
1 egg
1 Tbsp cornstarch
$\frac{1}{2}$ tsp salt
Dash pepper
Vegetable oil for deep-frying
Meatball sauce:
 1 Tbsp sugar
 1 Tbsp soy sauce
 $\frac{1}{2}$ Tbsp *mirin*

menu

Glazed Meatballs (see left)
Rice with Sprinkles
Scrambled Egg with Vegetables (see p 61)
Candied Sweet Potatoes (see p 76)
Agar-agar Jelly

Combine ground meat
and onion well, then add
all remaining ingredients.
Knead well until sticky, and
shape into 4 balls. Heat oil
to 340 °F (170°C) and deep-
fry, occasionally rolling, for
2-3 minutes. Heat sauce
ingredients in a saucepan and
add drained meatballs. Cook
and stir until the sauce is thick
and the meatballs are glazed.

Hint: Colorful food picks
will make cute skewers
making the slippery
meatballs easy to eat.

Nori Rice

$^2/_3$ cup (4 oz /115 g) warm rice, $^1/_2$ sheet *nori*, 1 tsp soy sauce, *Furikake* (rice sprinkles - see p 81)

Cut out shapes from *nori* sheet using a craft puncher and/or scissors. Place half portion of rice in bento box, and cover it with torn *nori* pieces dipped in soy sauce. Cover it with remaining rice, and add rice sprinkles. Arrange *nori* cut-outs.

Fried Chicken

3 oz (90 g) chicken thigh, 2 Tbsp each rice wine and soy sauce, $^1/_2$ Tbsp honey, $^1/_2$ tsp ginger juice, Salt and pepper, All-purpose flour, Vegetable oil for deep-frying

menu

Nori Rice (see right)
Fried Chicken (see below)
Tomato and Cucumber Skewers (see p 69)
Baby Apple Rabbits (see p 65)

NORI BENTO WITH FRIED CHICKEN

How to make Fried Chicken

1 Trim away excess fat from chicken. Cut into bite-size pieces.

2 In a plastic bag, put rice wine, soy sauce, ginger juice and chicken pieces. Lightly knead to mix the ingredients, and let stand about 10 minutes.

3 Drain excess moisture by placing chicken on paper towel, and coat the chicken pieces with flour. This process can be done using another bag.

4 Deep-fry in 340°F - 360°F (170°C - 180°C) oil until golden and crisp. Let cool to pack.

56

menu
Quick Fried Prawns (see below)
Simmered *Hijiki* **Seaweed** (see p 74)
Veggie Omelet (see p 61)
Bus Rice (see below)

Quick Fried Prawns
3 prawns, shelled and deveined
1 Tbsp each all-purpose flour,
mayonnaise and breadcrumbs
Parsley, minced

Authentic Fried Prawns
3 prawns, shelled and deveined
1 Tbsp all-purpose flour
$^1/_2$ beaten egg
2 Tbsp breadcrumbs
Vegetable oil for deep-frying

Bus Rice
$^2/_3$ cup (4 oz /115 g) warm rice, 2 slices
chikuwa (tubular fishcake – see p 81),
1 slice cooked ham, *Furikake* (rice
sprinkles – see p 81)

Place rice in bento box (of any shape.)
Make bottom half of bus body with rice
sprinkles. Arrange *chikuwa* (tubular
fishcake - see p 81) wheels and ham
windows.

Hint: Include a mini bottle of tartar
sauce mixed with a fair amount of
minced vegetables.

QUICK FRIED PRAWN BENTO

How to make Quick Fried Prawns

❶ Combine equal amounts of flour and
mayonnaise.
❷ Coat prepared prawns with the batter.
❸ Coat with breadcrumbs mixed with
minced parsley.
❹ In preheated toaster oven, lay aluminum
foil, and place prawns. Cook 4 minutes on
each side.

How to make Authentic Fried Prawns

❶ Pat dry prepared prawns, and coat with flour.
❷ Dip in beaten egg.
❸ Coat with breadcrumbs leaving the tails uncoated.
Deep-fry in medium hot oil until golden.

ROLLED MEAT VARIATIONS

Spread 1 oz (30 g) thin slice of beef (sirloin), and roll string beans and carrot strips inside the meat.

BEEF

Spread 1 oz (30 g) thin slice of pork loin, and roll frozen potato fries and ketchup inside the meat.

PORK

Spread 2 oz (60 g) chicken breast slice, and butterfly to flatten thick part. Place pickled plum paste and *shiso* leaf on it, and roll up.

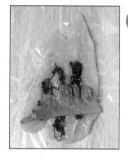

CHICKEN

STUFFED BEEF ROLL BENTO

menu
Stuffed Beef Rolls (see below)
Molded *Onigiri* (see p 12)
Asparagus and Cherry Tomato Skewers
Baked Sweet Potatoes (see p 76)
Strawberry

Stuffed Beef Rolls
2 thin slices beef sirloin
$1/4$ onion
$1/2$ Tbsp each soy sauce and *mirin*
Dash cornstarch, salt and pepper

Cut onion into thick slices, and sauté briefly. On a flat surface, spread beef and sprinkle with salt and pepper. Place sautéed onion slices near you, and roll up. Secure rolled end with a dash of cornstarch. Sauté rolls in a heated frying pan. Add soy sauce and *mirin*. Shake the pan until the beef rolls are glazed.

Rolled Pork with Mushrooms (see below)
Potato Salad (see p 72)
Rice with Sprinkles
Cherry Tomato
Cheese Balls (commercial)
Satsuma

Rolled Pork with Mushrooms

2 thinly slices pork loin
²/₃ oz (20 g) *enoki* mushrooms
¹/₂ Tsp each soy sauce and rice wine
Dash cornstarch

Spread a pork slice, and trim *enoki* mushrooms to the width of the pork. Roll tightly and secure the end with cornstarch. Sauté in a heated frying pan. Add soy sauce and rice wine. Shake the pan until lightly browned.

> **Hint:** Pork dishes go well with sweet flavors, try rolling apple slices sautéed in butter in them.

STUFFED PORK ROLL BENTO

FRIED CHICKEN SPIRAL BENTO

Fried Chicken Spirals

3¹/₂ oz (100 g) ground chicken,
4" (10 cm) green onion, chopped,
¹/₄ beaten egg, 1 Tbsp *miso*,
Dash ginger juice, rice wine,
cornstarch and sugar, ¹/₂ sheet *nori*,
1 slice cheese

1. In a bowl, combine ground chicken, green onion, ginger juice, beaten egg, *miso*, sugar, rice wine and cornstarch. Knead well until sticky.
2. Spread chicken mixture over the *nori*, and top with a slice of cheese. Roll up pressing the near end of *nori* into chicken mixture to form a scroll.
3. Cook in a greased frying pan, rolling occasionally over medium heat. Cover and reduce heat. Cook until heated through completely.

Red *Shiso* Rice

Mix ²/₃ cup (4 oz /115 g) warm rice and 2 tsp *yukari* (red *shiso* sprinkles - see p 81). Place in bento box, and arrange sweet pea center, *kamaboko* (steamed fishcake, stick type) petals and pea pod leaves and stem.

menu

Fried Chicken Spirals (see left)
Sautéed Pasta (see p 68)
Red *Shiso* Rice (see left)
Strawberries

> **Soboro Rice**
> Make 4 kinds of *soboro*, or sprinkles, and spread over rice. Separate strips of imitation crab stick and make "borders," if preferred.

menu
Soboro Rice (see below)
Sautéed Carrots (see p 68)
Curried Cauliflower (see p 70)
Cheese Ball

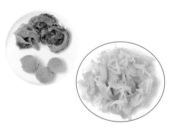

SOBORO BENTO

Beef *Soboro*	4 oz (120 g) ground beef, 1½ Tbsp soy sauce, 1 Tbsp each *sake* and sugar

In a saucepan heat all the seasonings to boiling. Add ground beef and stir vigorously with 2 pairs of chopsticks or fork, to separate into fine pieces. Cook and stir until the liquid is absorbed.

Egg *Soboro*	2 eggs, 1 Tbsp sugar

Put eggs and sugar in a saucepan. Stir constantly using 2 pairs of chopsticks or fork, over low heat. Continue stirring until dry scrambled egg is formed. Immediately remove from the pan.

Salmon *Soboro*

Cook salted salmon fillet, and crumble into fine flakes. Salmon flakes are available in jars.

Scallop *Soboro*

Cook scallops with dash of *sake*, soy sauce and sugar to taste. Break into flakes.

SWEET OMELET VARIATIONS

VEGGIE OMELET

Roll with thawed vegetable mix.

HEART SHAPED OMELET

Slice rolled plain omelet. Slice in half diagonally. Turn over one half to form a heart shape. Secure with a food pick.

CRAB STICK OMELET

Roll with imitation crab sticks (see p 81).

How to make Rolled Omelet

1 Beat 2 eggs and add 1 Tbsp sugar and a dash of salt.

2 Grease well-heated frying pan with vegetable oil. Remove from heat, and pour a half portion egg of mixture. When the surface is half set, start rolling.

3 Roll up, and then slide the roll towards the other end. Pour remaining egg mixture, and repeat rolling.

How to make Regular Omelet

1 Pour egg mixture into a frying pan, and stir as you would with scrambled eggs over easy (half cooked) over high heat.

2 Push the mixture to one side of the pan and cook just until the surface is lightly browned.

3 To preserve the shape, roll up with plastic wrap, and squeeze lightly. A perfect shape will be created.

KAWAII BENTO ACCENTS

Just one little addition makes a difference and adds fun at lunchtime. Here are some cute attention getters and convenient space fillers. Use a hole punch to cut out *nori* rounds.

QUAIL EGGS   CHICKEN EGGS   SAUSAGES   KAMABOKO   VEGETABLES   APPLES

QUAIL EGGS

CHICK

❶ Using a paring knife, make zigzag slits only into egg white.

❷ Remove top. Press black sesame seeds and a piece of cut out carrot onto yolk (to make eyes and beak).

PIGLET

Dye boiled quail egg with yellow food coloring, and press on black sesame seeds, carrot cutouts, and an instant fried noodle for tail.

SMILING SUN

Dye boiled quail egg with red food coloring, and press on black sesame seeds and a piece of red pepper for a mouth. Insert instant fried noodle pieces around edges.

DARUMA DOLL

Dye boiled quail egg with pink food coloring, and peel away circle for face and pattern on front. Press on black sesame seeds to make eyes and eyebrows.

STEMMED CHERRIES

Dye boiled quail eggs with red food coloring, and insert a parsley stem cut into letter V.

CHICKEN EGGS

RACOON DOG

Dye boiled egg by soaking in soy sauce. Attach sausage tail, sliced cheese eye section, and *nori* muzzle. Stick black sesame seeds for eyes.

WILD RABBIT

Dye boiled egg by soaking in soy sauce. Attach carrot ears/eyes and *nori* nose.

MINI FRIED EGGS

Drop quail eggs into bell pepper rings sliced into ¼" (5-6 mm) width. Remove some egg white so as not to brim over when cooked. Fry to your favorite doneness.

SAUSAGES

OCTOPUS

Slit end of red sausage to make 8 tentacles before cooking until they spread. Attach black sesame seed eyes and *nori* strip headband.

CRAB

Split a sausage lengthwise. Make 3 slits into each side. Make tiny slits to hold eyes of black sesame seeds. Cook to shape.

FLORETS

Using a paring knife, cut into sausage making deep zigzag slits. Separate pieces and squeeze out a dash of ketchup onto each center. Trim bottom ends flat.

BEETLE

Using short plump sausage, make wings by scoring a letter T. Make horn with narrow sausage, and attach to body by connecting with a piece of instant fried noodle. Attach sesame seed eyes and noodle legs. Cook to shape.

STAG BEETLE

Using a regular sausage, make wings by scoring letter T. Make horns with zigzag cut sausage, and connect to body with instant fried noodle pieces. Attach sesame seed eyes and noodle legs. Cook to shape.

SUNFLOWER

Split sausage lengthwise in half. Make deep slits along one side (do not cut through). Join ends with wooden toothpick. Place in frying pan, and drop egg yolk of quail egg. Cover and cook until done (see p 12.)

KAMABOKO

Kamaboko (steamed fishcake - see p 81)

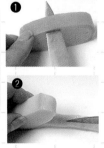

RABBITS

❶ Slice into ⅜″ (1 cm) width. Make ears by inserting knife ⅛″ (3 mm) under the colored top and work until ⅔ is separate.
❷ Turn over, and make deep slits into separate strip. Turn over again and fold down split parts to make ears.
❸ Attach eyes of black sesame seeds.

DECORATIVE ROPE

❶ Work the same as Step ❶ of "RABBITS"
❷ Turn over and make a short slit along center of each strip. Pull end of strip through the slit just made, and turn over again.

BUTTERFLY

Slice into ⅜″ (1 cm) width. Trim away letter V on colored side. Lay flat and slice in half widthwise, leaving end still attached. Spread open, and attach patterns with string bean slices, cheese and *nori*.

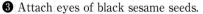

VEGETABLES

RADISH FLORET

Score crisscross on top, and trim away sides. Score 2 lines on each side. Soak in cold salted water until "petals" open.

MUSHROOM

Trim bottom of radish flat. Scrape off round patterns all around. For stem, trim away top and bottom of boiled quail egg or fresh mushroom stem.

 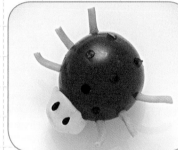

WALL CLOCK

Arrange black sesame seeds on thinly sliced radish. Make hands with parsley stems (not necessarily 3 o'clock!)

LADYBUG

Use cherry tomato for body, and attach *nori* patterns. Insert legs of instant fried noodles. Make head with cheese ball cut in half, and attach sesame seed eyes.

SALAD CASE

Choose bell pepper which "sits" still. Cut off top half, and remove inside. Fill with salad of your choice.

❶ Insert a sharp pointed paring knife into center of 1½ - 2" (4 - 5 cm) length of cucumber. Work zigzag, thrusting knife deep into the core.

❷ Hold both ends, and carefully pull apart.

CUCUMBER FLORETS

With a paring knife, slit and separate a cut section of cucumber. Separate and place *umeboshi* (pickled plum) paste or bell pepper cutout in center.

BROCCOLI MONSTERS

Cook broccoli florets in salted boiling water. Add eyes of cut-out cheese and *nori*, and voila!

CHERRY TOMATO FLORET

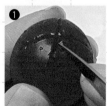 

❶ Using a sharp pointed paring knife, score six sections by making three even cuts.

❷ Peel skin halfway, pulling to open out. Attach corn kernel to center.

CAULIFLOWER LAMB

Choose a plump section of cauliflower, and cook in salted boiling water. Attach boiled shrimp "horn" and carrot face with sesame seed eyes. Insert pretzel stick legs.

APPLES — 4 Apple Shapes

APPLE LEAVES

Insert knife along side edges on both sides. Cut deep enough to separate large center section.

BASIC WEDGE

Cut into 8 wedges, and remove cores.

BABY APPLE RABBIT

Cut in half.

APPLE TULIP

Score zigzag line along cut side.

Cut into the center section, insert knife in the same manner to separate next center section.

APPLE RABBIT

Score a letter V.

Score letter V on cut side.

Peel to the end of scored line.

Repeat until smallest center section is a narrow leaf shape.

Peel to the end of scored line.

Peel to the end of scored line.

Using knife as if peeling, score tulip leaf line on both sides.

Pull centers apart to create a pattern, and dip in salted water to prevent discoloring.

Dip in salted water to prevent discoloring.

Dip in salted water to prevent discoloring.

Dip in salted water to prevent discoloring.

APPLE LEAVES

APPLE RABBIT

BABY APPLE RABBIT

APPLE TULIP

BENTO FAVORITES CLASSIFIED BY COLOR

Assorting colors of food items is a good way to
menu from a nutritious point of view. Here are

STRING BEANS WITH SESAME DRESSING

3-4 string beans, 1 Tbsp
toasted sesame seeds, 1 tsp
soy sauce, 1 tsp sugar, Dash
salt

1. In ample boiling water, add a
dash of salt, and blanch the string
beans.
2. Drain in a colander, and cool
under running water. Drain and
slice diagonally.
3. Combine sesame seeds, soy
sauce and sugar to make dressing,
and mix with the string beans.

SPINACH WITH BLACK SESAME DRESSING

2 oz (60 g) spinach, 2 tsp
ground black sesame seeds,
$^1/_2$ tsp soy sauce, $^1/_2$ tsp sugar,
Dash salt

1. Wash spinach and put in a
plastic bag, without shaking off
water. Microwave 30 seconds.
Immediately blanch in cold water;
drain and cut up. Squeeze out
water.
2. In a small bowl, combine ground
sesame seeds, soy sauce and sugar.
Add spinach and mix well. Drain
before packing.

CHEESY SPINACH

1 oz (30 g) spinach, 1 slice
cheese, Dash salt,
$^1/_2$ tsp butter

1. Wash spinach and put in a
plastic bag, without shaking off
water. Microwave 30 seconds.
Immediately blanch in cold water;
drain and cut up. Squeeze out
water.
2. In a preheated frying pan, heat
butter and sauté spinach.
3. Sprinkle with salt, and add
torn cheese slice. Stir briefly and
remove from heat.

SAUTÉED GREENS

1 *komatsuna* greens or bok choy
2 imitation crab sticks (see p 81)
$^1/_2$ tsp sesame oil
Dash salt

1. Wash *komatsuna* and put in a
plastic bag, without shaking off
water. Microwave 30 seconds at
500W. Immediately blanch in cold
water; drain and cut up. Squeeze
out water.
2. Cut crab sticks in half lengths,
and tear randomly.
3. In a preheated frying pan, add
sesame oil, *komatsuna* and seafood
sticks. Sauté briefly and sprinkle
with salt.

BACON-ROLLED ASPARAGUS

1 stalk asparagus, 1-2 slices
streaky bacon, $^1/_2$ tsp white wine,
Dash salt, $^1/_2$ tsp vegetable oil

1. Cut asparagus into bite-size
pieces. Roll each with bacon and
secure the end with a wooden
toothpick.
2. Heat vegetable oil in a frying pan,
and cook rolled asparagus pieces
seam sides down. Turn and cook all
sides.
3. Sprinkle with wine and salt. Omit
salt if the bacon is salty. Remove
wooden toothpicks and insert
decorative picks.

WAKAME AND CUCUMBER WITH VINEGAR

$^1/_4$ Japanese cucumber, 1 tsp
dried *wakame* seaweed,
Vinegar dressing: 1 tsp vinegar, 1 tsp
sugar, Dash salt and soy sauce

1. Soak dried *wakame* in water until
soft. Squeeze out water and blanch
in boiling water until the color turns
green. Cool in cold water, cut up and
squeeze again.
2. Slice cucumber thinly and sprinkle
with salt. Let stand until supple, and
squeeze out water.
3. Combine vinegar dressing
ingredients and mix with *wakame*
and cucumber slices. Leave a while
to drain before packing.

judge the completeness of the
reminders to design your bento.

BROWN/BLACK   WHITE   YELLOW   RED   **GREEN**

BEEF AND PEPPER STIR FRY

1 oz (30 g) lean beef, thinly
sliced, 1 bell pepper, 1 oz
(30 g) bamboo shoot, 1 tsp oyster
sauce, 1 tsp rice wine, $^1/_2$ tsp
soy sauce, 1 tsp cornstarch,
1 clove garlic, minced, $^1/_2$ tsp
vegetable oil

1. Shred beef and dust with
cornstarch. Shred bell pepper and
bamboo shoot likewise. Combine
oyster sauce, rice wine and soy
sauce.
2. Heat oil and minced garlic in a
frying pan. When the garlic releases
aroma, add beef and stir-fry until
heated through. Remove beef.
3. Add pepper and bamboo shoot
slices, and stir-fry 1 minute. Put back
beef, and add combined seasonings.
Stir until the sauce is absorbed.

COLESLAW

1 cabbage leaf, $^1/_4$ Japanese
cucumber, 1" (2.5 cm) carrot,
1 Tbsp French dressing, 1 tsp
mayonnaise, Dash salt

1. Slice cabbage and carrot into
fine shreds.
2. Slice cucumber in half
lengthwise, and then into thin slices.
Sprinkle salt over cucumber slices,
and let stand until supple; squeeze
tightly.
3. In a bowl, combine everything
excluding salt. Let stand a while to
drain before packing.

Note: Add canned sweet corn, if
preferred. Drain well so as not to
make the coleslaw soggy.

STEWED CELERY

$^1/_2$ stalk celery, $^1/_2$ tsp bouillon
granules, Scant $^1/_4$ cup water,
Dash soy sauce, 2 Tbsp dried
bonito shavings

1. Peel celery, and cut the lengths
according to the bento box.
2. Bring scant $^1/_4$ cup water to
boiling with bouillon granules and
cook celery pieces 3-5 minutes
until fork tender and the liquid is
absorbed.
3. Sprinkle with soy sauce and
turn off heat. Sprinkle with bonito
shavings. Let cool in the pan to let
the flavor penetrate.

BROCCOLI WITH SALTY *KOMBU*

3 florets broccoli, $^1/_2$ Tbsp
shio kombu (dusted shredded
kombu), Dash salt

1. Cook broccoli in ample boiling
water with a dash of salt just until
the broccoli turns fresh green.
Drain and let stand to cool.
2. Toss with shredded *kombu*. Leave
until the *kombu* pieces are soft, and
the salt is absorbed in the broccoli.

SPINACH WITH *NAMETAKE* MUSHROOMS

1 oz (30 g) spinach, 2 tsp
nametake (simmered *enoki*
mushrooms sold in a bottle)

1. Wash spinach and put in a plastic
bag, without shaking off water.
Microwave 30 seconds.
Immediately blanch in cold water;
drain and cut up. Squeeze out water.
2. In a bowl, combine spinach and
nametake mushrooms. No seasonings
are necessary as the *nametake* does
the job.

OKRA WITH BONITO SHAVINGS

2 pods fresh or frozen okra,
$^1/_2$ tsp soy sauce, Dash salt,
2 Tbsp dried bonito shavings

1. In salted boiling water, cook
okra only briefly. If using frozen
okra, just blanch in boiling water
and drain. Blanch in cold water,
and slice.
2. In a bowl, combine okra, bonito
shavings and soy sauce.

Note: Bonito shavings can hold
moisture and prevent leaking from
the bento box.

GLAZED CARROTS

3 mini carrots, ¹⁄₂ Tbsp sugar, 1 tsp butter, 1 parsley sprig

1. Peel carrots. In a small saucepan, put carrots and water to cover, and heat to boiling.
2. Add sugar and butter, and reduce heat to low. Cook until the liquid is gone.
3. Using a toothpick, make a hole into each top of the carrot, and insert a parsley sprig to resemble carrot leaves.

Note: If using a thick carrot, slice thickly and cut out shapes with cookie cutter.

SAUTÉED CARROTS

¹⁄₄ (2"/5 cm) carrot, 1 tsp sesame oil, Dash sugar, salt and toasted white sesame seeds

1. Peel carrot and cut into matchsticks.
2. In a preheated frying pan, heat sesame oil, and stir-fry carrot pieces. Sprinkle with sugar and salt to taste. When heated through (do not overcook), add toasted white sesame seeds to finish.

Note: This is a carrot version of *Kimpira* (page 75), a popular companion of rice in Japan. Carrots can be cut into thin rectangular or round slices. Cut out shapes with a cookie cutter before slicing for a fun *kimpira*. Make a large batch and save for later use.

CARROT SALAD

¹⁄₄ (2" /5 cm) carrot
Dash salt, 2 tsp raisins
1 Tbsp French dressing
Dash honey

1. Finely shred carrot, and sprinkle with salt. Leave until carrot becomes supple, and squeeze out water.
2. In a bowl, combine carrot, raisins, French dressing and honey.
3. Let stand a while and squeeze out moisture before adding to bento box.

COD ROE AND JELLY NOODLES

1¹⁄₂ oz (40 g) salted and cured cod roe, 2 oz (60 g) *shirataki* (fine white yam noodles), 1 tsp vegetable oil, Dash salt and soy sauce

1. Remove skin of cod roe. Wash *shirataki* and cut into 3" (8 cm) lengths.
2. In a frying pan, heat oil and add *shirataki*. Stir-fry over high heat until it makes a sizzling sound.
3. Add cod roe and stir quickly to separate the eggs evenly. Add salt and soy sauce to adjust the taste.

SAUTÉED PASTA

1 oz (30 g) pasta, ¹⁄₈ red bell pepper, 2 Tbsp ketchup, 1 tsp butter, Dash salt

1. Cook pasta in ample amount of salted water; drain.
2. Mince red bell pepper.
3. In a frying pan heat butter and stir-fry bell pepper. Add ketchup and pasta, and sprinkle with salt to adjust the taste.

EASY MIXED *TEMPURA*

2 Tbsp *sakura-ebi* (dried pink shrimp), 2 Tbsp *tempura* flour or all purpose flour, 1 Tbsp water, Vegetable oil for deep-frying

1. Make batter by combining flour and water well. Add dried shrimp and mix.
2. Heat ample oil in a frying pan or wok. Using a teaspoon, drop a small amount of the mixed batter. When the surface becomes dry, turn and fry until crisp. Drain on paper towel.

HAM STUFFED CHERRY TOMATOES

3 cherry tomatoes
1 slice honey roast ham

1. Choose tomatoes with nice stem ends. Wash and cut off top part to make a "lid". Using a knife and spoon, scoop out inside of tomatoes.
2. Cut ham into ⅜" (1 cm) wide strips, and roll 2 strips to fill the tomato.

Note: Be sure to remove excess moisture from the inside of tomatoes.

SAUTÉED RED BELL PEPPER

¼ red bell pepper, ½ tsp vegetable oil, Dash salt

1. Cut bell pepper into 2" (5 cm) long slices.
2. Heat vegetable oil and stir-fry the bell pepper slices.
3. When the pepper becomes supple, sprinkle with salt to taste.

TOMATO AND CUCUMBER SKEWERS

3 cherry tomatoes
2" (5 cm) cucumber

1. Remove stem ends of the tomatoes before washing.
2. Slice cucumber into about ⅜" (1 cm) thicknesses, and cut out a shape using a cookie cutter. Lightly sprinkle with salt.
3. Dry cucumber pieces with paper towel. Skewer cherry tomatoes and cucumber shapes alternately.

TARAMO SALATA

1 oz (30 g) salted and cured cod roe, 1 small potato, ½ tsp butter, 1 Tbsp mayonnaise

1. Remove skin of cod roe, and combine well with mayonnaise to make a paste.
2. Peel potato and cut into about 1" (2.5 cm) cubes. Cook in ample water until soft. Discard water, and bring back to heat, stirring constantly to dry the potato cubes.
3. In a bowl, mash the cooked potato, and add butter. Lastly add cod roe paste and mix well.

SHRIMP IN CHILI SAUCE

1 oz (30 g) shelled shrimp, Dash cornstarch and rice wine, ⅛ onion, minced, 1 Tbsp vegetable oil
Combined seasoning:
2 Tbsp ketchup, 1 Tbsp water, 1 tsp each sugar and cornstarch, ½ tsp Chinese stock granules, Dash tobanjan (Sichuan bean paste)

1. Wash shrimp and put in a small bowl. Add a dash of rice wine and cornstarch. Rub to coat the shrimp evenly.
2. In a heated wok or frying pan, add vegetable oil and stir-fry shrimp. Remove shrimp and cook minced onion. Put back shrimp, and add combined seasoning at once. Cook and stir until the sauce has thickened.

CHEESE STUFFED TOMATO TRIO

3 cherry tomatoes,
Cream cheese, Sliced cheese,
Ricotta cheese

1. Choose tomatoes with nice stem ends. Wash and cut off top part to make a "lid." Using a knife and spoon, scoop out inside of tomatoes.
2. Cut sliced cheese into ⅜" (1 cm) wide strips, roll tightly and insert into one tomato. Using a spoon, fill another tomato with cream cheese, and another with ricotta, making sure they are tightly packed.

Note: Be sure to remove excess moisture from the inside of tomatoes.

CURRIED CAULIFLOWER

2 oz (60 g) cauliflower, 1 tsp vinegar, 1/4 tsp curry powder, Dash salt

1. In a small bowl, combine vinegar, curry powder and salt.
2. Separate florets of cauliflower, and cook in boiling water until done, but still crisp.
3. Drain in a colander, and add to the bowl of seasonings. Mix well to coat the surfaces of cauliflower evenly.

SWEET POTATO DUMPLING

2 oz (60 g) peeled sweet potato, 1 tsp raisins, 1 Tbsp sugar

1. Wash and peel sweet potato to remove fibrous edges. Slice into about 1/2" (1.5 cm) rounds, and immediately soak in water 3 minutes to prevent discoloring.
2. Boil sweet potato until fork-tender. Remove from heat and discard water. In the saucepan, mash the potato.
3. While hot, mix in sugar and raisins. Spoon an appropriate amount onto a plastic wrap, and bring all sides together. Twist the top to form a dumpling.

APPLE SWEET POTATOES

2 oz (60 g) sweet potato, 1/2 tart apple, 1/2 Tbsp sugar, Dash lemon juice, 1 tsp honey

1. Wash sweet potato and cut into bite-size pieces. Soak in water to prevent discoloring.
2. Cut apple into wedges. Trim off core, and slice into 1/2" (1.5 cm) thicknesses. Sprinkle with lemon juice.
3. Put sweet potato, apple and sugar in a saucepan, and add water to barely cover. Cook over medium heat to boiling. When sweet potato becomes tender, reduce heat and continue simmering until there is no moisture. Add honey and stir.

SIMMERED SWEET POTATOES

2 oz (60 g) thin sweet potato, 1 *kuchinashi* (gardenia fruit /dried herb to dye bright yellow color), placed in a gauze bag (optional), 3 Tbsp sugar, 1/2 tsp each salt and soy sauce

1. Wash skin of sweet potato, and slice into 1/2" (1.5 cm) skin-on rounds. Soak them in water at least 30 minutes.
2. Put drained sweet potato pieces and *kuchinashi* in a saucepan; add water to cover, and heat to boiling over high heat.
3. Reduce heat to low, and add sugar, salt and soy sauce. Simmer until the sauce has just gone.

FRIED QUAIL EGGS

3 curried quail eggs (see p 71), Cornstarch for dusting, 1 Tbsp flour all purpose flour, 2 Tbsp water, Breadcrumbs, Oil for deep-frying

1. Make curried eggs referring to page 71, and drain.
2. Dust drained quail eggs with cornstarch.
3. Coat each egg with flour, water, then with breadcrumbs.
4. Heat oil to low (325 °F/160℃) and deep-fry until golden.

BUTTERED SQUASH

2 oz (60 g) winter squash
1 tsp each sugar and butter
Dash of salt

1. Carefully peel squash, and cut into bite-size pieces.
2. Place pieces with sugar and salt in a saucepan, and add water to cover. Cook until nearly fork tender, add butter, and continue cooking over medium heat.
3. When the squash becomes tender and the moisture has almost gone, remove from heat.

SQUASH SALAD

1 oz (30 g) fresh or frozen winter squash, ¼ Japanese cucumber, Dash salt, ½ boiled egg, 1 Tbsp mayonnaise

1. Peel squash, and cut into bite-size pieces. Dip briefly in water, and wrap with microwave safe plastic wrap. Microwave 2 minutes until tender at 500W. If using frozen squash, microwave before peeling.
2. Slice cucumber thinly and sprinkle with ample salt. Rub salt onto cucumber slices, and leave 3 minutes: squeeze out moisture.
3. Cut up boiled egg, and combine with cucumber and squash in a bowl. When the heat reduces, mix in mayonnaise.

BUTTERED CORN EGG DROPS

2 Tbsp canned or frozen sweet corn, 1 beaten egg, Dash salt and butter

1. Drain canned sweet corn. If using frozen corn, thaw by microwaving 30 seconds (500W) in a microwave safe covered container.
2. In a frying pan, heat butter and sweet corn. Stir-fry briefly, and season with salt.
3. Drizzle in beaten egg, stirring to "bind" sweet corn.

Note: When in season, use fresh kernels of corn.

QUICK QUICHE

1 small wiener, 2 frozen French fries, 1 tsp frozen vegetable mix, 1 cherry tomato, 1 tsp shredded Mozzarella cheese, ½ beaten egg, ½ Tbsp milk, Salt and pepper

1. Cut up wiener, French fries and cherry tomato. Thaw frozen vegetables by microwaving 30 seconds at 500W.
2. In a small bowl, combine beaten egg, milk and pizza cheese, and adjust the taste with salt and pepper. Add wiener, fries and tomato to the bowl and mix well.
3. Pour the mixture into an aluminum cupcake set in a cupcake pan up to 80% to avoid overflowing.
4. Cover with foil, and bake 7-8 minutes in a toaster oven.

PINEAPPLE SALAD

1 slice canned pineapple, ¼ apple, 1 oz (30 g) cream cheese, 1 Tbsp plain yogurt

1. Cut pineapple into ½" (1.5 cm) pieces. Cut apple into wedges. Core and slice thinly.
2. In a bowl, combine cream cheese and yogurt. Add pineapple and apple slices, and mix well.

CURRIED QUAIL EGGS

3 boiled quail eggs, ½ bouillon cube, ½ tsp curry powder, ¼ cup water

1. In a microwave safe container, combine bouillon cube, curry powder and water.
2. To avoid "explosion" of the boiled eggs, pluck them with a pick, and put in the bowl of curry seasonings. Cover and microwave 1 minute at 500W.
3. Let cool, occasionally turning over for even coloring.

MARINATED YELLOW BELL PEPPER

¼ yellow bell pepper, Dash honey, French dressing

1. Cut bell pepper lengthwise in half, then slice thinly.
2. Combine French dressing and honey. Adjust the taste, and toss pepper slices with the dressing.
3. Marinate a while and drain before packing in the bento box.

GOBO SALAD

4" (1½ oz /40 g) *gobo* (burdock root), 2" (5 cm) carrot, 2 Tbsp mayonnaise, 1 Tbsp ground sesame seeds, Dash salt

1. Scrape off skin from *gobo*, and cut into matchsticks. Peel carrot and cut in the same manner.
2. In a saucepan, heat water to boiling, and cook *gobo* and carrot briefly just until heated through; drain well and let cool.
3. Toss with ground sesame seeds and mayonnaise. Adjust the taste with salt.

GERMAN POTATOES

1 small potato
1 strip bacon, cut up
½ tsp butter
Dash salt

1. Peel and slice potato into thin quarter rounds. Cover and microwave 2-3 minutes or just until tender.
2. Heat butter in a frying pan. When butter melts, stir-fry potato slices, and then add bacon slices.
3. Season with salt. (If moist finish is preferred, pour in some milk to finish)

FLUFFY POTATOES

1 small potato
Salt and pepper

1. Peel and cut potato into bite-size pieces. In a saucepan, boil in water to cover over medium heat until tender.
2. Discard water, and cook potato further, constantly shaking the saucepan until the surface of the potato pieces are dried and fluffy.
3. Sprinkle with salt and pepper to taste.

MACARONI SALAD

1 oz (30 g) pasta, ¼ Japanese cucumber, 2" (5 cm) carrot, 1 slice honey roast ham, 2 Tbsp mayonnaise, Dash salt

1. Cook pasta in ample salted water. Cut carrot into thin strips and add to the pot just before the pasta is soft. Drain and let cool.
2. Slice cucumber thinly and sprinkle with salt. Leave 3 minutes and squeeze to remove extra moisture. Combine cucumber, pasta, carrot and ham. Season with mayonnaise.

POTATO SALAD

1 small potato, 2 Tbsp frozen vegetable mix, ¼ Japanese cucumber, 2 Tbsp mayonnaise, Dash salt

1. Peel and cut potato into ½" (1.5 cm) cubes. Boil potato until tender, then add frozen vegetable mix to the pot to cook together. Discard water, and cook potato cubes further in the dry pot to release extra moisture. Roughly mash the potato cubes
2. Slice cucumber thinly and sprinkle with salt and leave 5 minutes. Squeeze to remove moisture, and mix with potato and vegetables, adding mayonnaise.

POTATO STIR FRY

1 oz (30 g) frozen French fries (shoestring), ½ cabbage leaf, Salt and pepper

1. Cut frozen fries into half lengths. Cut up cabbage.
2. In a heated frying pan, cook and stir frozen fries until browned. Add cabbage and continue cooking.
3. When the cabbage is supple, season with salt and pepper. (Use no oil as the frozen fries contain fat)

SAUTÉED *ENOKI* MUSHROOMS

½ pack (2 oz /60 g) *enoki* mushrooms
½ tsp butter
Dash soy sauce

1. Trim off root ends of *enoki* mushrooms. Cut length in half.
2. Heat butter in a frying pan, and cook *enoki* stirring constantly until the texture becomes supple. Sprinkle with a dash of soy sauce to taste.

KAMABOKO SANDWICHES

1" (2.5 cm) *kamaboko* (steamed fishcake – see p 81), 1 tsp low-salt *umeboshi* (pickled plum)

1. Slice fishcake in half thicknesses, and make a deep slit along the middle.
2. Shave off flesh of pickled plum (or use pickled plum paste). Insert pickled plum into each slit, and add *shiso* leaf, if preferred.

STUFFED FISHCAKE

1 *chikuwa* (tubular fishcake – see p 81), ½ Japanese cucumber

1. Cut cucumber lengthwise into quarters to make sticks. Scrape off corner edges using a peeler.
2. Insert into the hole of *chikuwa*, and cut diagonally into bite-size pieces.

BEAN-THREAD VERMICELLI SALAD

⅓ oz (10 g) dried bean-thread vermicelli, ¼ Japanese cucumber, 2" (5 cm) carrot, 2 imitation crab sticks (see p 81), 2 Tbsp soy sauce based salad dressing

1. Peel and slice carrot into fine julienne strips. Slice cucumber the same size.
2. Cook carrot in ample boiling water 2 minutes, then add bean-thread vermicelli cut into 2" (5 cm) lengths. Cook about 5 minutes or as directed on the package. Drain in a colander and pour tap water to cool; drain.
3. In a small bowl, combine all the ingredients and the salad dressing. Let stand a while, and be sure to drain moisture before adding to bento boxes.

BUTTER POTATO DUMPLING

1 small potato, 2 tsp sugar, 1 tsp butter, Dash salt, Raisins and apple peel for eyes and mouth

1. Peel potato and boil in ample water to cover over high heat. Bring to boiling, reduce heat and continue cooking until the potato is tender.
2. Discard water, and bring back to heat. Using a wooden spatula, quickly mash the potato until smooth, releasing extra moisture. Remove from heat.
3. Add sugar and butter. Mix well and spoon 1 Tbsp of mashed potato onto plastic wrap. Arrange raisins and apple peel cut into a triangle. Bring all sides of the wrap together, and twist on top.

SHIRA-AE (*TOFU*-DRESSED SALAD)

1 (3 oz /90 g) Chinese cabbage leaf, 2" (5 cm) carrot, 5-6 peapods, 1 tsp dried *hijiki* seaweed, soaked in water to soften, 5 oz (140 g) cotton *tofu*, 1 Tbsp toasted white sesame seeds, 1 Tbsp sugar, 2 tsp white *miso*

1. Cut Chinese cabbage into wide strips. Shred carrot and peapods. Bring water to boiling, and cook all the vegetables over high heat until the colors turn bright. Drain in a colander, and let stand to cool.
2. Wrap up *tofu* in paper towel. Place on a microwave safe plate, and microwave 1 minute at 500W.
3. Squeeze out moisture from *hijiki* and cooled vegetables.
4. In a bowl, combine *tofu*, toasted white sesame seeds, sugar and *miso*, until sticky. Add vegetables and *hijiki*, and mix well.
(Makes about 1 cup)

73

BENTO FAVORITES CLASSIFIED BY COLOR

SIMMERED *HIJIKI* SEAWEED

1 Tbsp dried *hijiki*, 1½" (4 cm) carrot, ¼ *aburaage* (*tofu* puff), ¼ cup reconstituted *dashi* stock, ½ Tbsp each soy sauce and sugar, ½ Tbsp vegetable oil

1. Rinse *aburaage* under boiling water to remove excess oil. Cut into julienne strips. Cut carrot likewise.
2. Heat sesame oil in a frying pan, and stir-fry carrot and drained *hijiki*. Add *aburaage*, then add water, *dashi* granules, soy sauce and sugar. Cook over low heat stirring occasionally until the sauce is almost gone.

SAUTEÉD AND SIMMERED LOTUS

2 oz (60 g) lotus root,
2 tsp. soy sauce, 1 tsp sugar
½ tsp toasted sesame seeds,
1 tsp sesame oil

1. Peel and slice lotus root thinly. Soak in water 10 minutes.
2. Heat sesame oil in a frying pan, and stir-fry drained lotus root slices over high heat. When they become transparent, add sugar and soy sauce, and keep stirring until there is no moisture and the slices are well glazed. (Leaving pan uncovered will assure crispness)
3. Sprinkle with roasted sesame seeds.

POTATO ROLLS

1 (2 oz /60 g) small potato,
3 strips (1½ oz /40 g) thinly sliced boneless pork rib, Salt and pepper

1. Peel potato and cut into thick julienne strips. Blanch in water and arrange on a microwave plate. Cover with plastic wrap, and microwave 1 minute at 500W.
2. Spread pork, and sprinkle with salt and pepper. Place a potato stick in the center of each and roll meat tightly around it. Roll the remaining sticks.
3. In a heated frying pan, begin cooking the rolls with the seam sides down. Turn until browned on all sides.

GROUND BEEF WITH *GOBO*

4" (1½ oz /40 g) *gobo* (burdock root), 2 oz (60g) ground beef, 1 Tbsp each sugar and soy sauce, 1 tsp sesame oil

1. Wash and slice *gobo* into thin shavings, and immediately soak in water ; drain.
2. In a non-stick frying pan cook ground beef until crumbled. Add *gobo* and stir-fry 1-2 minutes. When the *gobo* becomes transparent, season with sugar and soy sauce. Cook until the sauce is almost gone, and sprinkle with sesame oil.

NORI-WRAPPED *HAMPEN* AND CHEESE

½ *hampen* (steamed fish product),
1 slice cheese,
⅛ sheet *nori*, cut into strips

1. Cut *hampen* into bite-size pieces. Cut cheese to fit into *hampen*. Make a deep slit into each *hampen*, and insert a cheese piece.
2. Wrap a *nori* strip around the middle of the *hampen* sandwich. Cook in a non-stick frying pan until browned, turning once.

Note: Use cheese stuffed hampen, if available.

STUFFED *SHIITAKE* MUSHROOMS

2 *shiitake* mushrooms
1 Tbsp canned tuna
1 Tbsp mayonnaise
2 Tbsp mozzarella cheese
Dash ketchup, if desired

1. Clean and trim *shiitake*, and grill 1-2 minutes in a preheated toaster-oven.
2. Combine tuna and mayonnaise, and fill the *shiitake* caps. Add a little ketchup, and top with cheese.
3. Grill 3-4 minutes until the cheese melts.

SQUASH BALLS

1 oz (30 g) winter squash, ¹/₂ tsp black sesame seeds, Salt to taste

1. Cut squash into chunks. Blanch in water, and arrange on a microwave safe plate. Cover and microwave 2 minutes at 500W.
2. Remove hard skin while hot, and mash roughly. Spoon onto plastic wrap. Gather and squeeze ends of the wrap to form a ball. Remove wrap and sprinkle with sesame seeds.

WAKAME AND SARDINES

1 tsp dried *wakame* seaweed, 2 tsp *chirimen jako* (dried baby sardines), Dash sesame oil and fresh ginger juice

1. Soak *wakame* in water to soften. Drain and cut up.
2. Heat sesame oil in a frying pan, and stir-fry *wakame* and baby sardines

FRIED *TOFU TERIYAKI*

¹/₄ cake *atsuage* (thick fried *tofu*), 1 tsp each soy sauce and sugar, Dash vegetable oil

1. In a bowl, blanch *atsuage* with boiling water ; drain to remove excess oil. Cut into bite-size pieces.
2. Heat oil in a frying pan, and add *atsuage* pieces occasionally turning to brown the sides. Finish with soy sauce and sugar, stirring to coat all the *atsuage* pieces.

KIMPIRA

4" (1¹/₂ oz /40 g) *gobo* (burdock root), 2" (5 cm) carrot, 1 Tbsp each sugar and soy sauce, Dash sesame oil and toasted sesame seeds

1. Wash and cut *gobo* into 2" (5 cm) long julienne strips. Immediately soak in water. Cut carrot likewise.
2. Heat sesame oil in a frying pan, and stir-fry carrot and drained *gobo* over high heat. When the *gobo* turns transparent and supple, stir in sugar and soy sauce to taste. Stir constantly until there is no moisture left.
3. Sprinkle with sesame seeds.

CHIKUZEN-NI (BRAISED CHICKEN AND VEGETABLES)

¹/₄ lb (115 g) chicken thigh, 1 (7 oz /200 g) carrot, 4 oz (115 g) each lotus root, *gobo* (burdock root) and bamboo shoot, 5-6 (6 oz /170 g) taros, 2-3 dried *shiitake* mushrooms, soaked and softened in water, ¹/₄ cake *konnyaku* (yam jelly), 2 Tbsp each sugar and soy sauce, 1 cup reconstituted *dashi* stock including *shiitake* soaking water

1. Wash and peel taros. Sprinkle taro with salt, and rub with your hand to remove jelly-like substance (this is to help seasonings to seep well) Cut all the ingredients into bite-size pieces.
2. In a saucepan, heat 1 cup stock and all the ingredients except taros. Check doneness with *gobo* by piercing with a fork, and if it goes through, add taros and sugar and soy sauce to taste. Simmer until the sauce is almost absorbed. (Makes 3 - 4 servings)

KOREAN SALAD

1 oz (30 g) each soybean sprouts, cooked royal fern, cooked spinach, and carrot, 2-3 pieces black mushrooms (ear fungi) soaked and softened in water, ¹/₄ tsp salt, 1 tsp each sesame oil and toasted white sesame seeds, Dash soy sauce and grated fresh garlic

1. Cut all the ingredients into about 2" (5 cm) lengths. Cut carrot and mushroom into thin julienne strips.
2. Heat ample water to boiling. Add a dash of salt, and then put the ingredients in order: carrot, bean sprouts, mushrooms, and then royal fern. Lastly add spinach and remove from heat.
3. Drain in a colander, spread to let cool evenly. Squeeze them tightly to remove moisture. Combine all the seasonings in a small bowl, and toss the vegetables.

QUICK DESSERT IDEAS

Ingredients here are for an easy to cook batch. Use what you need and save the rest for later use.

BAKED SWEET POTATOES

10 oz (300g) sweet potato, 2 oz (60g) butter, 2 oz (60g) sugar, 1 beaten egg, ¼ cup whipping cream

1. Peel sweet potato thickly to remove fibrous edges. Cut into chunks and boil until fork tender.
2. Drain well and put back into the pot. Mash roughly and mix in sugar and butter while hot. Mash until smooth and stir in beaten egg and cream. Keep stirring until a dough forms.
3. Put the paste in a piping bag, and pipe into cupcake papers.
4. In a preheated toaster-oven, bake 7-8 minutes until top is browned.
(Makes 8 - 10 with 1½" (4 cm) muffin cups)

CHEESE CUPCAKES

8 oz (230 g) cream cheese, ½ cup whipping cream, 1 egg, ⅓ cup (2 oz /60 g) sugar, 4 slices canned pineapple, minced, Cookies for crust

1. Leave cream cheese at room temperature until soft. Beat cheese until light and fluffy, and beat in cream, beaten egg and sugar. Beat until smooth. Add pineapple pieces.
2. Line muffin cups with crushed cookies. Pour dough into each. In a preheated toaster oven, bake 7-8 minutes until partially browned. (Wrap each in a plastic wrap and keep frozen for later use.)
(Makes 8 - 10 with 1½" (4 cm) muffin cups)

CANDIED SWEET POTATOES

1 (10 oz /285 g) sweet potato, 2 Tbsp sugar, Toasted black sesame seeds (optional), Oil for deep-frying, 1 tsp vegetable oil

1. Peel sweet potato, and cut into random wedges (cut diagonally as you roll). Soak in water 10 minutes to prevent discoloring. Drain and dry with paper towel.
2. Heat deep-frying oil to medium (325°F-340°F/160°C-170°C). Deep-fry potato pieces until they float to the surface.
3. In a small saucepan, heat 1 tsp oil and sugar until sugar has melted and bubbly. Add fried potato pieces at once, and remove from heat. Stir quickly so potato pieces are evenly covered. Sprinkle with sesame seeds if preferred. Do not overheat as the sugar can scorch easily.
(Makes 4 - 5 portions)

FRIED SESAME DUMPLINGS

½ cup glutinous rice flour, Scant ½ cup water, ¼ cup (2 oz /60 g) adzuki bean jam, 3-4 Tbsp white sesame seeds (raw), Oil for deep-frying

1. Place rice flour in a bowl, and add water gradually while kneading until the texture resembles a soft bread dough. Divide the dough into quarters and roll each into a ball.
2. Quarter bean jam and roll into balls. Press one ball of dough flat, and wrap a bean jam ball in it. Seal the top. Roll between your palms to form a perfect ball. Make 4 and coat with sesame seeds. Heat oil to low (325°F /160°C), deep-fry 4-5 minutes until golden.
(Makes 4)

FRUIT SALAD

½ cup (2 oz) of tiny bits of apple, kiwi, strawberry, orange, banana (Canned fruit cocktail can be used), 2 Tbsp cottage cheese, 1 Tbsp plain yogurt

1. Cut fruits into bite-size pieces, and wrap them in a paper towel to remove extra moisture.
2. Combine cottage cheese and yogurt well. Mix in the minced fruits. Put in a tightly sealed container.
(Makes 2¼ cups)

MILK JELLY

¾ cup milk, ¼ cup water, 2 Tbsp sugar, 1 tsp (1/12 oz /2 g) agar-agar powder

1. In a small milk pan, heat water and agar-agar to boiling until the agar-agar has completely dissolved.
2. Reduce heat and add milk and sugar. Cook 2 minutes over low heat. Let cool.
3. Pour into molds and cool in a refrigerator.
(Makes 5 - 6 in ¼ -cup molds)

TOFU DUMPLINGS

¹/₈ cake (1 oz /30 g) silk *tofu*, ¹/₄ cup
(1 oz /30 g) glutinous rice flour,
¹/₂ Tbsp sugar, 2 tsp soybean flour
mixed with 1 tsp sugar

1. In a bowl, break *tofu* and gradually
stir in rice flour until as soft as a bread
dough. Add sugar and keep kneading.
2. Heat water in a saucepan to boil.
Pinch off the dough and roll into a ball.
Press your thumb into each center to
make a dent, and cook in the boiling
water.
3. When the balls float to the surface,
remove and cool in cold water. Drain and
dust with soybean flour and sugar mix.
Serve with maple syrup, if preferred.
These dumplings keep their softness for
hours.
(Makes 6 - 8)

QUICK COOKED APPLES

1 tart apple, 2 Tbsp sugar, 1 tsp
lemon juice

1. Wash apple thoroughly and cut
lengthwise into quarters. Remove core
and cut each in half. Then slice into ¹/₄"
(5-6 msm) in. thicknesses.
2. Place apple slices in a microwave safe
dish, and sprinkle with sugar (let stand
until the sugar melts). Sprinkle with
lemon juice. Cover with plastic wrap and
microwave 1 minute and 30 seconds at
500W. Adjust cooking time according to
your oven.
3. Heat the pan over low heat. Add
lemon juice, and cook until there is no
liquid left.
(This also makes a tasty filling for
sandwiches or pancakes. Add cinnamon
if preferred)
(Makes about 3 portions)

ALMOND TOFU

³/₄ cup milk, ¹/₄ cup unsweetened
condensed milk, 2 Tbsp sugar,
1 tsp (¹/₁₂ oz /2 g) agar-agar, Few
drops almond extract, Sugar syrup
made of ¹/₄ cup each sugar and
water, Fruits

1. In a small saucepan, place milk and
condensed milk. Turn on heat and add
sugar and agar-agar. Heat to boiling and
continue to cook 2 minutes over low heat
until the agar-agar is completely dissolved.
2. Remove from heat and add a few
drops of almond extract. Pour into a
shallow mold or container, and let cool.
Refrigerate until set. Make sugar syrup
by heating the same amount of sugar
and water; let cool.
3. In a tiny airtight container, arrange
cut fruits and almond tofu. Pour over
sugar syrup.
(Makes 5 - 6 portions)

JELLIED MANGO

¹/₂ ripe mango (6 oz /170 g flesh),
1 Tbsp lemon juice, 3 Tbsp sugar,
1 cup water, 1 tsp (¹/₁₂ oz /2 g)
agar-agar powder

1. Cut mango into cubes. If using frozen
mango, thaw before cutting. Sprinkle
with lemon juice and let stand a while.
2. In a small saucepan, heat water and
agar-agar to boiling ; reduce heat and stir
in sugar. Continue cooking 2-3 minutes
over low heat. Remove from heat and
add remaining lemon juice.
3. Add mango pieces and stir gently.
Pour into molds. Let cool in refrigerator.
(Makes 5 - 6 in ¹/₄ -cup molds)

JELLIED SATSUMA

¹/₄ cup canned Satsuma, 2-3 Tbsp
syrup from the can diluted with water
to fill 1 cup, 2 Tbsp sugar, 1 tsp (¹/₁₂
oz /2 g) agar-agar-powder

1. In a small saucepan, place agar-agar
and half of the syrup water. Heat to the
boiling point and cook 2-3 minutes over
low heat.
2. When the agar-agar is thoroughly
dissolved, add remaining syrup water,
and remove from heat. Let cool, and add
Satsuma. Pour into molds, and let cool
until set.
(Makes 5 - 6 in ¹/₄ -cup molds)

QUICK CUSTARD SAUCE

3 Tbsp each flour, milk, heavy
whipping cream, and sugar,
1 egg yolk

1. Place flour evenly on a microwave
safe plate. Microwave the flour 1 minute
to enhance the flavor.
2. In a milk pan, mix egg yolk with
sugar. Then add flour, and stir until
creamy.
3. Gradually stir in milk and cook over
low heat until bubbly. Remove from heat
and gradually stir in cream. Stir gently
until the texture is smooth. Cover and let
cool in the pan.

Note: Be sure to use agar-agar for bento lunches. Jellies made from gelatin often melt at room temperature while agar-agar jelly, once set, keeps its shape.

PICNIC BENTO

A picnic is a tradition that is enjoyed by all cultures. Here are some ideas from just three of them. Use your imagination to create one that incorporates ethnic foods that are familiar to you.

JAPANESE STYLE BENTO

menu (Clockwise from left)

Fried Prawns (see p 57)
Rolled Omelet (see p 61)
Shira-ae (*Tofu*-dressed Salad, see p 73)

Sekihan **Rice Balls** (see p 49*)
Onigiri, **or White Rice Balls**

Chikuzen-ni (**Braised Chicken and Vegetables**, see p 75)
Simmered Sweet Potatoes (see p 70)
Kamaboko **Sandwiches** (see p 73)
Decorative Rope *Kamaboko* (see p 63)

Rice Balls
*Make small oval-shaped rice balls with *sekihan* and plain rice, either with your hands or rice mold.
These rice balls contain no filling in order to enhance the flavors of all these dishes.

WESTERN STYLE BENTO

Fried Chicken Drumsticks

10 chicken drumsticks, All-purpose flour for dusting, Vegetable oil for deep-frying

Marinade: 3 Tbsp soy sauce, Scant $\frac{1}{2}$ cup apple or orange juice, Grated garlic

In a plastic bag combine marinade ingredients and chicken wings. Marinate overnight in a refrigerator. Pat dry chicken wings and coat with all-purpose flour. Deep-fry over medium heat until the outside is crisp.

Hint: For quicker marinating, use a fork to prick all over the chicken before soaking in the marinade.
For quicker deep-frying, precook in microwave oven.
Arrange chicken evenly on a plate and microwave 2 minutes (at 500W), and then deep-fry just until crisp.

79

CHINESE STYLE BENTO

menu (Clockwise from left)

Beef with Green Pepper Stir Fry (see p 67)

Sticky Rice and Chicken in Bamboo Leaves (commercial)

Almond Tofu (see p 77)

Spring Rolls (see below)
Egg Fu Yung (see p 23)

Shrimp in Chili Sauce (see p 69)
Jellyfish and Cucumber Salad (see below)
Cherry Tomatoes

Spring Rolls

7 oz (200 g) sliced pork, 1 bunch garlic chives, 1 can bamboo shoot, 8 spring roll wrappers, 2 Tbsp oyster sauce, 2 tsp cornstarch dissolved with 1 Tbsp water, Vegetable oil for frying

Cut pork, garlic chives and bamboo shoot into about 1" (2.5 cm) julienne strips. Heat oil in a frying pan, and stir-fry pork until heated through. Add bamboo shoot and then garlic chives. Stir in oyster sauce. Lastly stir in dissolved cornstarch to thicken. Let cool and wrap with spring roll wrappers. Deep-fry in 360°F (180℃) oil until crisp.(at 500W), and then deep-fry just until crisp.

Jellyfish and Cucumber Salad

Soak 2 oz (60 g) shredded and salted jellyfish (available in Oriental markets) in water 30 minutes at least to remove excess salt. Then soak in hot water around 140°F (60℃) to let shrink and soften. Shred $\frac{1}{2}$ Japanese cucumber and sprinkle with salt. Let stand until supple, and squeeze out moisture. Mix squeezed jellyfish and cucumber with 2 Tbsp rice vinegar, 1 Tbsp each sugar and soy sauce, $\frac{1}{2}$ tsp sesame oil and dash of mustard.